THE KENNEDY MYSTIQUE

CREATING CAMELOT

THE KENNEDY MYSTIQUE

CREATING CAMELOT

ESSAYS BY JON GOODMAN
Featuring commentary by Hugh Sidey,
Letitia Baldrige, Robert Dallek,
and Barbara Baker Burrows

NATIONAL GEOGRAPHIC
Washington, D. C.

TABLE OF CONTENTS

CONTRIBUTORS

HUGH SIDEY covered John Fitzgerald Kennedy as a reporter for *Time* and *Life* magazines. He wrote *Time* magazine's popular column "The Presidency" from 1966 to 1996. Over the course of more than four decades, he became one of America's foremost observers of the Oval Office. Hugh Sidey died in 2005.

LETITIA BALDRIGE was Jacqueline Kennedy's social secretary and was responsible for the lovely state dinners that characterized the administration. She is the author of 19 books, 14 of which concern manners and entertaining. A former assistant to the ambassadors of France and Italy, she was the first woman executive of Tiffany & Company. Since 1964, she has run Letitia Baldrige Enterprises.

ROBERT DALLEK is one of the most highly regarded historians in America today, winner of the Bancroft Prize and numerous other awards. He is the author of *An Unfinished Life: John F. Kennedy 1917-1963* and a widely acclaimed two-volume biography of Lyndon Johnson.

BARBARA BAKER BURROWS, the picture editor of *Life*, has had an association with the magazine and many of the world's foremost photographers for more than 35 years. She has edited some of the biggest stories of our time, including the Apollo space program and the Presidency. She has curated numerous exhibits and edited a large number of books.

THIS BOOK IS DEDICATED TO HUGH SIDEY.

INTRODUCTION

BY HUGH SIDEY

There was no precise moment when John Kennedy understood that the entry into the world of presidential power was through the lens of a 35-mm camera and television's portacam. But it occurred to all of us who were riding along on JFK's singular journey sometime in 1960 as we watched the world's best photojournalists descend on the candidate. Kennedy climbed from a marginally known U.S. senator who was unusually photogenic but not nationally known, with a huge and wealthy family, to a driving and charismatic star in the campaign firmament.

It would be a mistake to suggest his rise was due totally to image, because John Kennedy was a solid thinker and man of substance who sought results in politics. A lot of wealthy, handsome young men have tried their hands at a political career with little purpose and less intelligence, and in almost all cases they have been brushed aside.

But it would also be a mistake not to understand the huge importance of imagery in our age of pervasive communication. Long before there was a ringing Inaugural challenge, "Ask not what your country can do for you— ask what you can do for your country," or a Peace Corps, or the successful resolution of the mortally dangerous Cuban missile crisis, there was a Kennedy profile with a strong jaw and thick thatch of hair, and a straight arm that chopped at the air, and a rasping voice echoing across America, "Let's get this country moving again." That was the Kennedy who engaged millions of politically indifferent Americans.

He was in our time a fresh political entity among the old bourbons in both parties, and he was something beyond the glitzy surface celebrity we were accustomed to from the Hollywood machine; he was a man who championed youth and action and thought and courage, and he had seen and lived the horrors of battle and then turned to face the harsh winds of the Cold War following World War II. The revelation of the man of deep feelings and understanding of the exercise of world power came later.

The Kennedy family was not a stranger to the art of creating national images. Joseph P. Kennedy, the family patriarch, had gathered much of his fortune in Hollywood, making and distributing movies, hobnobbing with the stars and the people who manufactured screen glamour. The film industry was a staple of discussion at the Kennedy table in Massachusetts. The stars often mixed with the family. John Kennedy liked both the great stories produced on film and the people in them. Though there is not a record of him looking over the distant horizon and figuring how that knowledge would help put him in politics, the techniques of promotion and celebrity lay fallow in his mind, ready to be naturally infused in the great campaign of 1960.

Though *Life* and *Look* magazines were great fixtures in American life by the time Kennedy began to rise, and their intimate photo-essays of events and people were familiar, the 35-mm camera revolution that the magazines had wrought had not penetrated political reportage. The idea of a photographer with his tiny cameras following a candidate up close, not only recording the great rallies but going into the candidate's office and home and without restraint taking thousands of pictures, was beyond the tolerance of those old warriors like Harry Truman and Dwight Eisenhower. Politics and the political entourage up to Kennedy's time preferred the bulky Speed Graphic camera and the set photo session at a convenient time and place, and then three shots and out.

Television was by the late 1950s coming on strong, but here again the old-time pols were still frightened by its immediacy and irrevocability. The beloved President Ike would not risk a live television press conference until near the end of his eight years in the White House. Mistakes and bumbles made on live television were almost impossible to erase from the public mind. Kennedy, comfortable in his looks and his knowledge of the issues and his strength of speech, sought out the cameras when he could and was an eager promoter of the televised debates with Richard Nixon in the presidential campaign. In the first debate, an ailing and uncomfortable Nixon won on debating points, but the confident, tough, and handsome Kennedy won with the television audience. Many experts believe that that encounter was the beginning of Kennedy's campaign surge which took him to victory.

It was all second nature to Kennedy, really a natural part of his private and public life. Don Wilson, a former *Life*

HUGH SIDEY CONFERS WITH PRESIDENT KENNEDY IN THE OVAL OFFICE.

magazine staffer who joined the Kennedy campaign as a press aide, cannot remember that Kennedy ever sat down and designed a strategy for taking advantage of the photographers who by then were pestering for more and better pictures. It just happened. Kennedy swept them up in his travels and allowed them into his private life, never worrying about his appearance or political activity. He knew the facts of American life better than anyone around him, and as well as those others seeking the nomination, Hubert Humphrey, Adlai Stevenson, Stuart Symington, Lyndon Johnson, and Henry Jackson. And of course he was realist enough to know that, as press aide Wilson put it, "there was never a bad picture taken of John Kennedy."

There is a story behind the full flowering of those devastatingly compelling pictures of John and Jacqueline Kennedy and of the rest of the family— seven women including in-laws, and brothers Bobby and Teddy. Jacques Lowe, a young freelancer from New York, came to Washington to cover the rackets hearings, featuring big labor's defiant leaders Dave Beck and Jimmy Hoffa of the Teamsters Union. Bobby Kennedy was chief counsel for Senator John McClellan's committee, and as the chief inquisitor of the suspected bad guys, he was center stage asking the questions. Lowe scrambled around with the other photographers who had to work from below the committee table. As was his practice, Bobby, who by then was also planning his brother's run for the Presidency, used to scoop up reporters and photographers and take them for interludes of touch football and picnics at his Virginia estate, Hickory Hill.

Lowe relished the outings. To pay Bobby back he shot pictures of the Kennedy family, who were always engaged in athletics or horseplay. Bobby was so taken with Lowe's candid shots he asked for 124 of the 11x14 prints to give to his father for his 69th birthday. Old Joe, as he was called by then, proclaimed those pictures the best birthday present he had ever received, and he asked Lowe to do the same thing for Jack and Jackie Kennedy.

Kennedy then was running for re-election to the Senate and gearing up for the presidential campaign that would follow his sure Senate victory. Jack and Jackie were as taken with Lowe's work as the other Kennedys. Lowe suddenly found himself as the inside Kennedy photographer. In the following three years he would produce many of the famous images that live on today and can be found in this book.

Kennedy was not totally oblivious of how he looked for the hordes of cameramen, who by the spring of 1960 were gathering around his primary campaign. The demand from print editors and television producers for intimate pictures had increased manyfold. Kennedy preened a bit. On a couple of occasions I dropped in at his Senate office when he was getting a haircut, his thick hair having become a focal point for fashion arbiters. The barber furnished Kennedy a hand mirror and went to work—carefully. It was rather a painful experience, with Kennedy issuing orders of

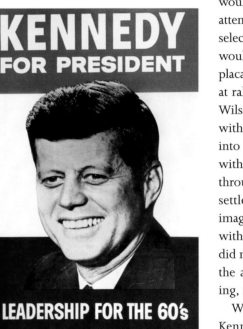

CAUTIOUS ABOUT THE IMAGE HE WOULD PROJECT, JFK CAREFULLY DELIBERATED OVER HIS 1960 CAMPAIGN POSTER.

where to cut and how much, so that it came out just right, not too close and with plenty of bush on top.

There was one moment of important deliberation about the Kennedy imagery that occurred after JFK won the nomination in July 1960. The Republicans and some Democrats had portrayed Kennedy as being too young and inexperienced for the Presidency. Knowing that as soon as the Republican Convention ended in August there would be a great surge of national attention, Kennedy asked his staff to select a central campaign picture that would be printed on thousands of placards that would be the backdrop at rallies and along motorcades. Don Wilson, because of his years working with photos on *Life*, was asked to dig into photography files and come up with the ideal image. After looking through scores of pictures, Wilson settled on a three-fourths-frontal image of a smiling, youthful man with lots of hair and teeth. Kennedy did not like it. He thought because of the age issues he should be unsmiling, more thoughtful.

Wilson and Ted Sorensen, Kennedy's principal speechwriter and policy aide, argued that the stronger portrait would be of youth and vigor. Finally Kennedy ordered up two pictures that could be used on posters, and at his home on Cape Cod he put both of them in front of him. As Don Wilson remembered it, Kennedy sat for about five minutes staring first at one and then the other. Finally, he said, "OK, let's go with the young one." That image—and many others—would carry him into the White House.

CHAPTER 1

A New Relationship With the Camera

ohn Fitzgerald Kennedy emerged onto the national scene during an era of monumental change in American media. A onetime print journalist himself, he was the first President to embrace the growing medium of television, and he used both of these to fashion his image at home and abroad. Kennedy's 1960 presidential campaign seemed to usher in a new era in American political life—one in which good looks, charisma, and the powers of public persuasion were added to the list of necessary presidential attributes. John Kennedy was imbued with hearty helpings of all these traits, and a commanding grasp of how to use them to his advantage.

It is hard to underestimate the influence of family patriarch Joseph P. Kennedy on the future President's early political career. A self-made millionaire, Joe Kennedy was a powerful man with an intuitive understanding of public relations. His deep pockets, friends in high places, and instincts for influencing public perception were indispensable to his son. Joseph Kennedy had, in his life, been a shipyard manager, a bank president, a Hollywood producer, a Prohibition-era rumrunner, and a stock speculator. But his abiding love was politics. His own father, Patrick "P.J." Kennedy, served five terms in the Massachusetts Senate; and his father-in-law, John Francis "Honey Fitz" Fitzgerald, served as Boston's mayor, as a member of the Massachusetts State Senate, and as a congressman in the U.S. House of Representatives.

Though Joseph P. Kennedy would never be elected to public office himself, he became a force to be reckoned with in American politics after undertaking successful fund-raising efforts for Franklin D. Roosevelt. In 1938, he reached the pinnacle of his public service career:

appointment as Ambassador to Britain, the first Irish-Catholic ever to hold the post.

The plum appointment marked a watershed in the political fortunes of the Kennedy family. In the summer of 1939, young John Fitzgerald Kennedy, a Harvard College senior and Joseph Kennedy's second son, traveled to Europe. During a whirlwind six-and-a-half-month trip, young "Jack" Kennedy gained unique access to London powerbrokers simultaneously preparing for, and desperately trying to avert, war. For Jack, it was a close-up look at what he called "Europe on the Eve."

At his father's side, he dined with the Queen and attended the ascension of Pope Pius XII. He was present in the House of Commons when British Prime Minister Neville Chamberlain laid out the case for war with Germany; and just days later, when a German U-boat sank the British passenger ship *Athenia*, Ambassador Kennedy sent his son to interview and comfort the survivors. The experience was seminal for a young man trying to understand America's place in the world, and Jack finished his European sojourn with the makings of a solid topic for a required senior thesis at Harvard.

While his son's political imagination was being fired by firsthand observation of the ominous developments in Europe, Joseph Kennedy's political career was coming to an end. A staunch isolationist who argued for the appeasement of Hitler and against U.S. participation in a European conflict, Ambassador Kennedy had views that clashed head-on with those of the English people; with their soon-to-be wartime leader, Winston Churchill; and, in the end, with FDR. In 1940, he was forced to resign his ambassadorship to the Court of St. James's. But Joe Kennedy was not the kind of man to sit back, even to nurse his wounds. With his own political dreams thwarted, he began channeling his political ambitions through his sons.

LEFT: *Press photographers surround candidate Kennedy, Omaha, Nebraska, 1959.*
PREVIOUS PAGES: *High school students from 56 countries crowd the President with handheld cameras and good wishes, 1963.*

When Jack finished writing his thesis back at Harvard, his father purportedly sent the manuscript to his friend, Arthur Krock, Washington bureau chief for the *New York Times*. Critics charge Krock rewrote, or at least heavily edited, the work; others suggest that Time-Life founder Henry Luce, another Kennedy friend, arranged to have the manuscript polished up. Whether either story is true or not, Luce did pen the foreword, and in 1940 it was published under the title *Why England Slept*. Upon the book's release, Joe Kennedy purchased some 30,000 copies. Barely out of college, Jack Kennedy had become the author of a topical bestseller. In many ways, the fashioning of his image had begun.

Convinced the United States would soon become part of the conflict in Europe, Jack joined the Navy. In 1941, he took a desk job at the Office of Naval Intelligence in Washington, D.C., but being so far from the action did not appeal to his nature. Jack engineered a transfer to the Pacific, where he commanded the motor torpedo boat PT-109. On night patrol in the Blackett Strait in the Solomon Islands a fast-moving Japanese destroyer collided with his boat, shearing it in two. Two crewmen were killed, and Kennedy suffered a back injury that would plague him for the remainder of his life.

The balance of the *PT-109* story has become a part of American political legend. Clutching the straps of a wounded soldier's clothing between his teeth, Kennedy led his remaining crew on a three-mile swim to a small deserted island. He then returned to the darkened waters in search of help. He survived for five days on little more than coconuts, but eventually encountered a friendly Solomon Islander. With the man's help—and that of a note scrawled on a coconut—Kennedy and his men were rescued, and the future President's exploits made their way back to the United States: Kennedy was now a war hero.

BOSTON MAYOR JOHN FRANCIS "HONEY FITZ" FITZGERALD GREETS PRESIDENT WILLIAM HOWARD TAFT, 1909.

Back home in the States, Jack did a brief stint as a reporter for the International News Service. As a special correspondent, he covered the crucial Potsdam conference, and the San Francisco conference that established the United Nations. By the summer of 1945, shortly after the celebration of V-E Day, and while war still raged in the Pacific, Jack Kennedy once again traveled to Europe, this time filing pieces for the Hearst newspapers. He observed the postwar situation, economic conditions, and the mood of those who survived the devastation. Although Kennedy would not choose to pursue journalism as a career, he demonstrated that he possessed the skills and instincts of a reporter. Both would serve him well in his subsequent political career.

Joseph P. Kennedy had originally pinned his highest political hopes on his firstborn son, Joe Jr. But after Joe, a Navy pilot, was killed in action over Europe during the war, the burden of political accomplishment fell to Jack. It was a burden he willingly assumed. In 1946, Jack Kennedy announced he would run for Congress from the 11th Congressional District of Massachusetts—the seat his grandfather once held. Capitalizing on the PT-109 incident, Joseph Kennedy spent a great deal of money to reproduce and disseminate a *New Yorker* article about his son's wartime heroism. Worried that the *New Yorker* piece wouldn't reach a wide enough audience despite being written by family friend John Hersey, the elder Kennedy had it reprinted in the more widely read and circulated *Reader's Digest*. He arranged a trip to Hollywood, so his son could mix, mingle, and learn from the best image makers in the world.

Though still physically weak from his war injuries, Jack campaigned aggressively during the race. He ignored the Democratic Party machine in Massachusetts's 11th Congressional District, relying instead upon his family, college friends, and fellow Navy officers for campaign guidance and support. The strategy worked. At age 29, he garnered nearly double the votes of his nearest opponent in the primary; in the November election he overwhelmed the Republican candidate.

In his three terms in the House (1947–1953), Kennedy advocated for better working conditions, more public housing, higher wages, lower prices, cheaper rents, and more Social Security for the aged. But his political ambitions were bigger than the U.S. House of Representatives.

In 1952 he challenged popular incumbent Henry

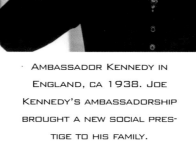

AMBASSADOR KENNEDY IN ENGLAND, CA 1938. JOE KENNEDY'S AMBASSADORSHIP BROUGHT A NEW SOCIAL PRESTIGE TO HIS FAMILY.

Cabot Lodge, Jr., for his Senate seat. Thousands of volunteers flocked to help, including his 27-year-old brother Robert, who managed the campaign. That fall the Republican presidential candidate, Gen. Dwight D. Eisenhower, carried Massachusetts by 208,000 votes; but Kennedy defeated Lodge by 70,000. At age 35, Jack Kennedy was well on his way to the top of the American political pyramid, a pinnacle he would reach in the company of a young woman who, in 1952, had recently taken a job working for the *Washington Times-Herald* newspaper.

While Jack Kennedy's political star rose, his future wife, Jacqueline Lee Bouvier, was cutting a memorable swath through society circles. The daughter of wealthy financier John Bouvier III and Janet Lee Bouvier, Jackie grew up in New York City and posh East Hampton, Long Island. Set upon a horse at the early age of one, within years she became an accomplished rider. In 1940, the *New York Times* reported Jackie's double victory in a horsemanship competition. Seven years later the Hearst newspapers would proclaim her Debutante of the Year.

Jackie attended the best schools, including Miss Porter's School for Girls in Farmington, Connecticut, Vassar College, and George Washington University in Washington, D.C. In the fall of 1951, she began her first job, becoming the "inquiring camera girl" for the *Washington Times-Herald*, taking photos and posing questions to Washington insiders on a wide array of topics.

In 1953, she interviewed two Senate pages about what it was like to observe senators at close range. Young

Jerry Hobbler of Ohio divulged, "[Kennedy's] always being mistaken for a tourist by the cops because he looks so young." To cover the story's opposite angle, Jackie turned to newly elected Vice President Richard Nixon and freshman Senator John F. Kennedy, asking them what it was like to observe the pages at close range. With characteristic humor, Kennedy quipped: "I've often thought that the country might be better off if we Senators and the pages traded jobs. If such legislation is ever enacted, I'll be glad to hand over the reins to Jerry Hobbler. In the meantime, I think he might be just the fellow to help me straighten out my relationship with the cops." Whether Jackie and the senator collaborated on this charming press clip is unknown, but the seeds of a relationship had been sown when the couple met at a Washington dinner party in 1951.

The same year the "inquiring camera girl" interviewed the witty freshman senator from Massachusetts for her column in the *Washington Times-Herald*, he asked for her hand in marriage. Their engagement was publicly announced with a cover story in *Life* magazine, which Joe Kennedy likely arranged. Always mindful of publicity, the couple actually withheld news of their engagement so as not to ruin another article about bachelor Senator Kennedy slated to run in the *Saturday Evening Post*.

The instantly iconic *Life* cover photo of the vibrant couple sailing on the senator's boat enchanted America. Photographs inside the magazine featured the photogenic pair frolicking in the sun and water around Hyannis Port, Massachusetts. They exuded a freshness and warmth that jumped right off the page, and they gave readers a couple to emulate. Jack and Jackie appeared supremely glamorous, yet somehow attainable. Picture-perfect images of them together struck an emotional chord in the American psyche, and the press.

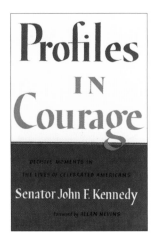

FEATURING PORTRAITS OF EIGHT U.S. SENATORS WHO RISKED THEIR CAREERS BY TAKING A STAND ON UNPOPULAR ISSUES, *PROFILES IN COURAGE* WON THE PULITZER PRIZE IN 1957.

The wedding of John Fitzgerald Kennedy and Jacqueline Lee Bouvier was one of the biggest spectacles of 1953. Some 3,000 people swarmed the church where the ceremony was held, eager for a glimpse of the "it couple"; and 1,200 invited guests, including quite a few members of the press, celebrated the union of two powerful Roman Catholic families at Hammersmith Farm, the Auchincloss estate in Newport, Rhode Island.

Shortly after the wedding, Jack's back problems took a turn for the worse and he was forced to undergo serious surgery. Aware that his previous writing paid high public relations dividends, while recovering Jack wrote a book highlighting the courage of eight distinguished senators. *Profiles in Courage* became a critical and commercial success, winning the Pulitzer Prize in 1957. And as good as he was at generating positive press, Jack Kennedy was fast becoming equally adept at dodging political bullets.

In Congress, Kennedy consistently supported the notorious anti-Communist Joseph McCarthy, another one of his father's friends. When McCarthy's paranoid charges of Communist infiltration in the government went too far and the Senate finally moved for his censure, Jack found himself in a pickle. His support of McCarthy threatened to become a political liability. Kennedy planned for the timing of the censure to coincide with one of his back surgeries, telling a friend his goal was to avoid any comment on the McCarthy matter. Kennedy's plan worked; he was never really called to account for his support of Joseph McCarthy.

Hard on the heels of Eisenhower's 1956 reelection victory, Kennedy set his sights on the 1960 Democratic presidential nomination. Young, inexperienced, and Roman Catholic, he had many strikes against him in the eyes of many party leaders. Nevertheless, he announced his candidacy early in 1960, and won seven primary victories by the time the Democratic National Convention opened in July. In West Virginia he won his most important victory, proving that a Roman Catholic could win in a predominantly Protestant state. Though he won the nomination, he faced a long, hard battle to reach the Oval Office.

From the beginning, the Kennedy campaign made it easy for reporters to cover the candidate, seeing to it that someone was always available to help journalists working tight deadlines. In a brilliant stroke, Kennedy's PR-minded staff began doling out instant transcripts of his speeches and remarks. This is standard operating procedure today, but in 1960 it was something most political campaigns simply didn't do. The transcripts were not only a defense against inaccurate quotes, but they were also a way to ensure being quoted often. The Kennedy campaign machine also released daily quotes to news outlets, so their candidate's bon mots stood a better chance of appearing in print with regularity. Kennedy also made deft use of the informal, old-school relationship between male reporters and male politicians where information was shared over scotch and cigars. Though more newspapers throughout the country ultimately endorsed his Republican opponent, Richard Nixon, Kennedy may have bested Nixon in the *amount* of coverage, something his campaign spared no cost—and worked with such precision—to secure.

Another campaign asset was Jacqueline Kennedy. Though tongues clicked over her spending on clothes, her intelligence and natural grace won over her critics. Photographs of Jackie—and adorable daughter Caroline—were soon in high demand.

The Kennedy-Nixon presidential debates are often cited as a turning point in the 1960 campaign. Knowing more about TV than his competitor, Kennedy wore the right makeup and suit. He looked ideal on camera. Nixon appeared haggard by comparison. Most Americans who tuned in to the debates on radio credited Nixon with victory, while those who watched on television identified the more attractive Kennedy as the winner. According to Theodore White's *The Making of the President 1960*, 6 percent of voters polled pointed to the debates as a deciding factor in choosing their new President. The number was crucial: Kennedy won the 1960 presidential election by a slim margin—112,000 votes.

Kennedy's narrow victory meant he had to continue to impress the American people. The vigorous campaigning done in the weeks and months leading up to Election Day could not be put behind him until he had convinced the country that he truly was the right man for the job. To quell remaining fears, Kennedy made the unprecedented decision to hold live press conferences. Just days after taking the nation's highest office, he was once again gambling on personal charm. When the notably conservative *Chicago Tribune* found out that the new President would be holding these conferences, it scoffed that Kennedy was attempting to establish a "government by public relations."

The *Chicago Tribune* may have been right, but so was Kennedy after all. Live press conferences became a presidential staple, and Kennedy would go on using charm, youth, energy, and natural good looks to mesmerize America. From the beginning, he would give people what they craved: greater access to the White House through increasingly off-the-cuff glimpses of their President. And as it turns out, the intimate portrait of John Kennedy painted in the media, on the cover of *Life*, and on television screens nationwide, would invigorate an American public increasingly proud of its fresh, youthful, and eloquent leader.

KENNEDY'S VICTORY AT THE 1960 DEMOCRATIC CONVENTION MADE THE COVER OF *LIFE* ON JULY 25.

IN THE PUBLIC EYE

Already a prominent businessman, Joe Kennedy became an international personality upon his appointment as U.S. Ambassador to the Court of St. James's in 1938. The British press embraced the large Kennedy clan, dubbing them the "nine-child envoy." The experience afforded John Kennedy the opportunity to travel throughout Europe as the clouds of World War II gathered, an experience that in turn inspired his Harvard thesis, titled *Why England Slept*. Published in 1940 with an introduction by *Time* and *Life* publisher Henry Luce, the book became a bestseller. Father Joe's early political aspirations rested on oldest brother Joe, a Harvard football star and Navy pilot. But Joe was killed when his plane exploded in August 1944 during a top secret mission to destroy the launchpad from which the Nazis were mounting their devastating attacks on London. It was the first of many public tragedies the family would endure.

LETITIA BALDRIGE: Joseph Kennedy's family served him well in his quest for power. When he was made ambassador, the whole family became instant movie stars in the eyes of the British public. And no one was prouder than Joe when his wife and two of his daughters were presented at court to the King and Queen. In a traditional ceremony, the Kennedy ladies, attired in white ballgowns, long white kid gloves, and white feathered headdresses, made well-practiced curtsies to Their Majesties. This was the social coup of all times for the Kennedy tribe.

ROBERT DALLEK: Joe Kennedy was a master of the art of public relations. In the midst of the Great Depression his wealth and large family of nine children made him a celebrity. His sons, John, Robert, and Teddy, learned that success as a public figure partly depended on mastering the art of public relations.

LEFT TOP: *July 2, 1938. Joe Kennedy with sons Joseph Jr. (left) and John (right) at Southampton, England.*
LEFT BOTTOM: *Dubbed the "nine-child envoy" by one British newspaper, members of the Kennedy family stroll on the embassy grounds in London.*
BELOW: *May 11, 1938. Kathleen (left), Rose (center), and Rosemary (right) prepare to be presented at court.*

LEFT: *John F. Kennedy sits with fellow PT-109 crew members. Paul "Red" Fay (right) would serve as undersecretary of the Navy during Kennedy's Presidency.*
ABOVE: *JFK pictured at a typewriter with his published thesis* Why England Slept.

HUGH SIDEY: Jack Kennedy lived his entire life in the shadow of war or as a participant in the real thing. That shaped his character, and his experience in battle was crucial in politics when the GI generation entered public life. The central theme of his Presidency was a search for peace and an agreement to control nuclear weapons. As a young man he watched the rising menace of Hitler from an often indifferent London, where his father, Joseph P.

Kennedy, was U.S. Ambassador. Then his boat, PT-109, was rammed and sunk in the Pacific and he became a true war hero, rescuing part of his crew. I once asked if he recalled the Great Depression, and Kennedy replied that the family's immense fortune had shielded him from economic hardship. "But I can tell you about the war," he replied. "That was my experience."

THE POLITICIAN

Following a brief stint as a reporter that took him to postwar Europe and San Francisco to cover the formation of the United Nations, Jack Kennedy, at age 29, set his sights on Massachusetts' 11th District Congressional seat. He worked long days campaigning through the mostly immigrant district, winning over voters with his earnest demeanor and backed by his father's wealth. He won the seat in 1946 and was reelected in 1948 and 1950. As a congressman he supported social legislation that benefited the working class and criticized what he considered to be the United States' weak stance against the communist Chinese government. After three terms in the House of Representatives, JFK set his sights on the Senate, defeating incumbent candidate Henry Cabot Lodge, Jr. in 1952.

LEFT: *Charlestown, Massachusetts, 1946. Twenty-nine-year-old congressional candidate John F. Kennedy campaigns at the Bunker Hill Day Parade.*

ABOVE: *Speaking to women voters at a series of teas was an essential part of Kennedy's 1952 Senate campaign.*
LEFT: *Senator Kennedy poses on the steps of the Capitol in this 1953 Arnold Newman portrait.*

BARBARA BAKER BURROWS: "The Senate" was the subject of Arnold Newman's 1953 story for *Holiday* magazine. As he playfully recalls: "The head of the Senate was a guy named Johnson. I photographed him, some senators and staffers, the most exclusive club in the world." Newman spent about three hours with Kennedy. It was the first time they had met, and he was not aware of any particular sense of destiny for the young congressman. However, Arnold photographed him in his "environment," a Newman specialty, adding an image of power to his subject's established good looks.

LETITIA BALDRIGE: John Kennedy turned the women of America to mush when they saw and heard him speak. He had an irresistible charm and a sex appeal. His appearances even at lightweight political gatherings, such as the tea parties hosted by the Kennedy family women, were probably key to his Senate victory and later to his presidential try. The women would rush home to persuade their husbands and boyfriends to "Vote for John F. Kennedy." A Republican candidate lamented, "How can we possibly win with all those gaga women working to elect him?"

INTRODUCING JACKIE

On September 12, 1953, John F. Kennedy wed Jacqueline Bouvier, a beautiful 23-year-old socialite who had attended the Sorbonne and was working as a roving photographer for the *Washington Times-Herald*. Their courtship made the cover of *Life* magazine in August 1953. The next month the same magazine followed up the story with photographs from their elegant wedding at Hammersmith Farm, the Auchincloss family estate in Newport, Rhode Island. More than 3,000 onlookers crowded St. Mary's Church in Newport to catch a glimpse of the handsome senator and his new bride. Reporting on the spectacle, *Life* presciently likened the event to "a coronation."

ABOVE: *Jacqueline Bouvier, ca 1951.*
RIGHT: *September 12, 1953. Crowds of people line the street outside Newport's St. Mary's Church to catch a glimpse of the newlyweds.*

LETITIA BALDRIGE: The wedding of Jacqueline Bouvier and John Kennedy preceded Princess Grace's wedding to Prince Ranier of Monaco, but the world had already decided that Jack and Jackie were the magical couple of the decade, and everything after was second best. The strong hand of Joseph P. Kennedy was seen everywhere in the management of the large wedding party, even though it was Jackie's parents who were giving the wedding. Someone remarked that the mob scene outside the church looked like the world premiere of *Gone With the Wind*. But there it was. The sign of the end of privacy for this pair ever after. They now belonged to the public.

BARBARA BAKER BURROWS: In the hands of Joe Kennedy, the wedding was an extravaganza. Warmed up by five days of partying at the Hyannis Port compound, the Newport ceremony and reception had all the trappings of a royal affair. The Archbishop of Boston read a special blessing from the pope, and the number of cases of champagne consumed was reported to the public. *Life* had no choice but to be there. And as the photographer representing America's preeminent magazine, Lisa Larsen had unmatched access. It was a marriage made in heaven: the Kennedys and *Life*.

YOUNG SENATOR

As television became an increasingly important medium in the 1950s, Senator Kennedy was quick to embrace the format, understanding its potential reach and impact on his public image. Although his performance on early television shows has been characterized as awkward, his natural demeanor seemed well suited to the medium. Despite his unsuccessful bid to become Adlai Stevenson's vice presidential candidate in 1956, Kennedy had by this time become a key media presence.

ABOVE: *An early appearance on CBS's* Face the Nation, *ca 1954.*
RIGHT: *May 9, 1954. Kennedy reads about the unraveling events in Indochina, an issue he would confront as a senator and later, as President.*
FOLLOWING PAGES: *Kennedy at work in his Senate office, 1957.*

HUGH SIDEY: Kennedy was the first presidential aspirant to understand the power and reach of the media complex—newspapers, magazines, radio, television, movies—which was frantically competing and growing and would engulf the political world. He was a book author, a speed-reader; for a short spell after World War II he was a foreign affairs correspondent for Hearst, and at one time thought he might like to publish a newspaper. The advent of television never intimidated him. Careful about his weight, his clothes, and abundant mat of hair, he was comfortable before any camera, and from his constant reading almost always knew more about public policy than those who questioned him.

ROBERT DALLEK: Kennedy had a keen sense of the importance of the media, particularly of television. In the fifties, he understood that TV would play a large role in shaping a politician's image. He also understood that his youthful appearance and attractive looks would give him an advantage over rival competitors for the Presidency. His success in his debates with Nixon in 1960 and his live televised press conferences—the first President to do this—vindicated his judgment.

THE PRIMARIES

It came as no surprise when John F. Kennedy announced his candidacy for the Presidency on January 2, 1960. For months he had traveled to every state in the union to build support and test the waters for his presidential bid. From the start, Kennedy was considered a long shot, far behind fellow Democratic hopefuls Hubert Humphrey and Lyndon Johnson. His youth, Catholicism, and wealth threatened to work against him. Supported by his hardworking network of family campaigning with him, Kennedy won important primaries in Minnesota and West Virginia. An impressive organized network supported the campaign, supplying reporters with the full text of the candidate's speeches to help facilitate their reporting. Kennedy's campaign would craft an environment of seemingly unprecedented access.

LEFT: *Seattle, Washington. John F. Kennedy speaks to a crowd early in his campaign.*
ABOVE: *Kennedy shakes hands with the crowd in Seattle.*

HUGH SIDEY: Jacques Lowe brought the 35-mm camera into the heart of the Kennedy family as the senator's presidential campaign was put into high gear. Such candid and intimate images had never been used before in high-power politics. The confident attractiveness of the people, the glamorous lifestyle, and the zest of the huge clan created an insatiable demand for Lowe's unprecedented photographs. The Kennedy legend was daily put on film and dispersed worldwide.

BARBARA BAKER BURROWS: Jacques Lowe first met JFK in August 1958. His earlier photographs of Bobby had impressed father Joe, and that assured him access to the candidate and his family. The results were more pictures and more intimate coverage by a young insider, a photographer who was often the only one there. Jack and Jackie both understood journalism. Having worked as a photographer, Jackie would ask Jacques about film speeds and the like—and that, too, helped guarantee a good personal look at the couple, skillfully focused on the image and the campaign.

LEFT: *Jacques Lowe photograph of JFK boarding his private campaign plane, renamed the Caroline for the presidential race*
BELOW: *Virtually anonymous in this 1959 Lowe photo, JFK and Jackie eat breakfast with brother-in-law Steve Smith at an Oregon diner.*

ABOVE: *April 1, 1959. John F. Kennedy speaks with Bishop G. Bromley Oxnam in Houston, Texas.*
RIGHT: *Charleston, West Virginia, April 1960. JFK walks with local supporters days before winning that state's primary.*

HUGH SIDEY: From the beginning, Kennedy understood that his Catholicism would be a major issue. No Catholic had ever been elected President. Kennedy rightly calculated that the old prejudices were easing and he faced the issue head-on, meeting with any religious group that asked. Before the Greater Houston Ministerial Association in the midst of the campaign, he defined himself. "I believe in a President whose religious views are his own private affair, neither imposed by him upon the nation or imposed by the nation upon him as a condition to holding office."

ROBERT DALLEK: Kennedy was masterly at appealing to Americans across class, ethnic, and racial lines. His privileged background—a son of one of the wealthiest families in America—did not set him apart from the mass of his countrymen. Although his Catholicism would initially limit his appeal to Protestant voters, his performance as President disarmed their suspicions and made him one of the most popular Presidents in the 20th century.

HUGH SIDEY: The media liked Senator Kennedy, and he returned the favor, which is a formula for at least a little favoritism and a lot of puffery for somebody who was often portrayed by the opposition as a too-young, too-inexperienced underdog up against the seasoned Richard Nixon with blessings from the immortal Ike. It soon became clear that publishers, as usual, favored Republican Nixon, but the working press, the campaign contingent, were pulling for Kennedy. They admired his intellect, his humor, and his unconventional campaign techniques, which above all included an easy access to himself. In his Senate years Kennedy had acquired a network of friends among reporters. He read their work, commented on it, both good and bad—the ultimate flattery for a writer. They were not social friends with the Jackie crowd, but professional friends, relishing the Kennedy caravan, which raced back and forth across the country, overtired but with a good story at every stop; sometimes even a new campaign speech and almost always a touch of humor.

Kennedy knew what he was doing; he knew too the editors and their prejudices, the media deadlines and demands. He held formal press sessions at most of his stops, but the rolling press interview was his genius. He would talk on the tarmac, aboard his plane the *Caroline*, at a lunch counter, or passing in a hall. He chose powerful newsmen, like those from the networks, *Time* magazine, and the *New York Times*, for special treatment back in his Senate office when he wanted to deal more in-depth with the big issues like the missile gap, his health, or religion. For most of the media it was a wonderful adventure, listening to, laughing with this young challenger. Almost from the beginning, despite fusty doubts from the top offices, the political reporters felt that Kennedy could actually beat Nixon, a powerful conviction that helped imbed the Kennedy mystique.

LEFT: *JFK holds an open-air press conference in Omaha, Nebraska, 1959.*
ABOVE: *Kennedy speaks with a reporter aboard a helicopter during a California campaign trip.*

IN FULL SWING

By the opening of the Democratic National Convention in July 1960, John F. Kennedy was a close candidate for the Democratic nomination. His campaign staff moved into high gear, setting up a 24-hour communication center from which they published a daily convention newspaper and monitored convention developments closely. The Los Angeles location suited Kennedy well; Hollywood friends Frank Sinatra and Tony Curtis came out in support of the candidate, amplifying his already glamorous image.

LEFT: *July 1960. Conventioneers wave Kennedy signs on the floor of the Democratic National Convention.*

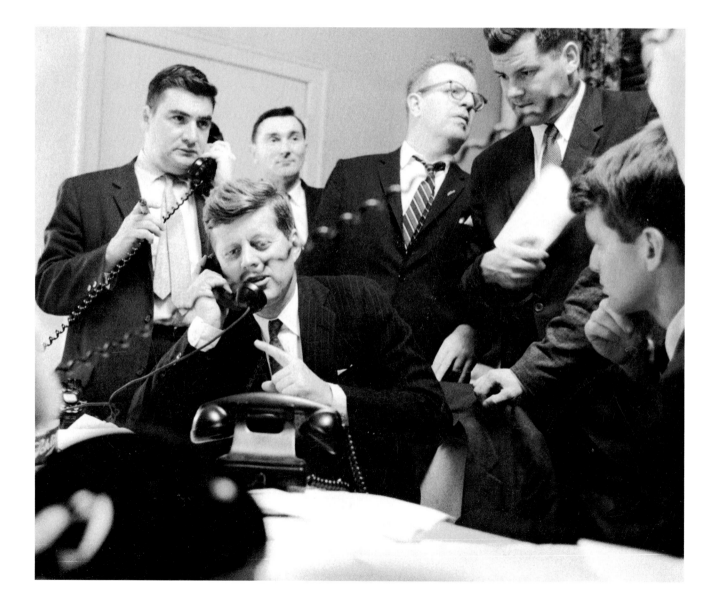

ROBERT DALLEK: Bobby Kennedy had honed his skills in his brother's earlier Senate campaigns in Massachusetts. He was tireless in organizing support for Jack's nomination and building an effective machine to turn out voters in the national contest against Richard Nixon. Some historians have credited Bobby with making the difference in Jack's narrow victory.

BARBARA BAKER BURROWS: In 1960, Jacques Lowe's photograph had all the trappings of a news picture: Only years later, after the public break between LBJ and the Kennedys, would Bobby's expression come to be more widely understood. It was another photographer, Hank Walker, who took a single frame of the Kennedy brothers conferring on the VP choice [p. 96], and kept to himself Bobby's muttered "shit, shit, shit." Photographers are supposed to have eyes, but not ears.

HUGH SIDEY: When the first debate was over it was estimated that 70,000,000 Americans had tuned in, one of the biggest audiences in television. Two men in a live broadcast answering unscripted questions from the media was, at least to the old-timers in politics, dangerous business. Not until the end of his eight years did Dwight Eisenhower allow a live televised press conference. Nixon and Kennedy were, however, eager for the encounter. Nixon was a renowned debater from school days. Kennedy, it was suggested, was less skilled, having a mediocre record on the Senate floor. But in the fall of 1960 the full impact of television was appreciated throughout the country and the handlers of both candidates swung into contentious action, arguing over the number of the debates (four were agreed to), the locality of the debates, the times, the placement, and stance of the participants—even the temperature of the room, since Nixon demanded high cooling because he tended to sweat under klieg lights. Briefing cards on the possible questions were prepared, dry runs were conducted, practices that would be enlarged and refined and continue to this day. Nixon was suffering from an injured knee and felt and acted weakened. Kennedy read his many newspapers, took a nap, and headed in the mellow September evening for the Chicago studio for the first debate. Kennedy looked confident, was feisty. Nixon looked sallow, as usual not sure what to do with his hands, but articulate and logical. Those who heard the debate on radio claimed that Nixon was the winner on substance. Those who watched television proclaimed Kennedy the clear champion. Political experts predicted the beginning of the end for candidate Nixon. The image was becoming all.

LEFT: *September 26, 1960. Presidential candidates Richard Nixon and John F. Kennedy square off in the first of four televised debates.*

ROBERT DALLEK: Kennedy was criticized during the presidential campaign for favoring symbol or image over substance. The journalist Eric Sevareid complained that Kennedy and Nixon were much the same: "junior executives on the make" without genuine political passion. There is some truth to this. Kennedy understood how important visual impressions were in a television age, and used his youthful appearance and handsome family to win voters to his side. But his victory over Nixon was the result of a lot more than manipulation of images. The country was demoralized at the end of Eisenhower's eight years. There was a lot of feeling that Soviet communism was surpassing the United States in technology and armaments. Kennedy capitalized effectively on these concerns in the campaign. He complained not only about "the missile gap" but also about the loss of confidence in the country's future. His promise of a "New Frontier" or commitment to get the country moving again in both domestic and foreign affairs went far to win him the Presidency.

BARBARA BAKER BURROWS: Like many images from Kennedy's campaign, there is much that is self-fulfilling about this photograph. It is not just the work of a photographer—many, including Life's Cornell Capa, brought their talents to capturing the moment. Rather, the message is in the event itself. The picture authenticates it. The scene in the photo at right is triumphal. It is as if, weeks before the election, the victor has been declared. For that, credit must go to the campaign; the reporters and photographers and their news organizations were handmaidens.

In a sense, every photo opportunity presents the editor with a similar predicament. Beginning years before the 1960 election campaign, the Kennedys created an image for the family and for the candidate. Partly a natural outgrowth from their accomplishments and lifestyle, it was enough to fascinate the press and public. But the special access granted to a handful of photographers in the run-up to the presidential election certainly helped to foster a very specific image. Obviously, Presidents had been photographed before their terms began, but never had the coverage been so orchestrated.

RIGHT: *New York City, October 19, 1960. JFK and Jackie are surrounded by a throng of supporters in a ticker tape parade.*

CHAPTER 2

Casting Images At Home & Abroad

Undeterred by the snowdrifts that forced Washingtonians to abandon their cars on the highways and the biting winds that made a 22°F day even colder, John F. Kennedy mounted the stage on January 20, 1961, to deliver his Inaugural Address without a hat or a coat. Seemingly inured to the cold, he intoned the words that would become well known to generations: "Let the word go forth from this time and place, to friend and foe alike, that the torch has been passed to a new generation of Americans"; and of course, "Ask not what your country can do for you—ask what you can do for your country." As the youngest President in American history deftly explained the ambitions and lofty ideals of his administration, it seemed that a new era was dawning in America.

Both John and Jackie recognized the importance of the occasion and showed their respect for it in their dress and behavior. With the help of *Vogue* editor Diana Vreeland, Jackie designed her Inaugural gown in white, which she felt was the most ceremonial color. Because of her delicate health following the one-month-early birth of second child John Jr., Jackie was home in bed early on Inaugural night. But Jack made it to all five Inaugural Balls, and Washington seemed to glitter with Hollywood glamour—from Frank Sinatra's pre-Inaugural gala for his pal Jack, to the scores of celebrities and political bigwigs decked out in white ties, tails, and top hats.

The new President didn't waste any time getting down to business. Early on, the administration decided to hold live press conferences. The idea was unprecedented—and risky. Live television left little room for error. From the State Department auditorium and his own desk in the Oval Office, Kennedy addressed the American public more than a dozen times during his first few months in office, announcing Cabinet appointments and keeping America informed about the workings of the New Frontier. His gamble paid off. Even if Washington insiders still considered him inexperienced, the public began to see Kennedy as the light and hope for a new era; and his frequent appearances on television helped to increase the profile of the Presidency. After all, it was much more effective to show close-ups of one man delivering remarks and commenting on developments around the country than to tell the entire story of a congressional battle or legislative debate. One news story after another emphasized to viewers that in Washington, President Kennedy was the man in charge.

As Letitia Baldrige expertly summed it up: "By fortune of the era or by lucky accident, the Kennedys were the first who were able to really manipulate the television for their use…. And everybody had to see it." Inviting glimpses of their personal lives in newspapers, magazines, and on television fostered a sense of intimacy between the Kennedys and America that had an almost palpable effect. From the very beginning of his short stay in office, Kennedy strove for a direct connection with the American people. Having won the election by such a slim margin, he knew that he had to continue to seduce the public at home, as well as abroad.

One message that Kennedy sought to convey to America, especially to young people, was that one person could make a difference in the world. On March 1, 1961, the new President announced the creation of the Peace Corps. The volunteers who would give their time to build homes, plan irrigation systems, erect schools, dig wells, or provide medical care, broadcast an image of energy, youth, and altruism to skeptics around the

LEFT: *January 20, 1961. President Kennedy on Inauguration Day.*
PREVIOUS PAGES: *January 20, 1961. The President and First Lady ride to the Inauguration.*

world, providing stores of goodwill the U.S. needed during the tensions of the Cold War. The message—that any young person could save people or communities and even, in their own small way, save the world— caught on. In two years, the program skyrocketed from 500 to 5,000 workers. The Peace Corps demonstrated the best of America to foreign countries through the energetic people who would give their time, sweat, and ingenuity to aid others. Their very presence abroad would help to combat the real threat of developing countries falling under the sway of communism.

Another program de-signed to combat commu-nism abroad, as well as advance goodwill in Latin America, was the Alliance for Progress, a long-term part-nership that would empha-size reform and develop-ment. In an East Room speech to congressional leaders and ambassadors from Western Hemisphere nations, Kennedy called on "all people … to join in a new Alliance for Progress—

THE NEW PRESIDENT AND FIRST
LADY LEAVE THE WHITE HOUSE
TO ATTEND THE FIRST OF FIVE
INAUGURAL BALLS.

Alianza para el Progreso—a vast cooperative effort, unparalleled in magnitude and nobility of purpose, to satisfy basic needs of the American people for homes, work and land, health and schools—*techo, trabajo y tierra, salud y escuela.*" The President's Spanish was far from flawless, but his attempt to speak to the ambassadors in their native tongue, as well as his offer of support, was a small step in the right direction in Latin American rela-tions. Historian Arthur Schlesinger wrote that Kennedy truly believed that the "American influence in the world depended less on American arms than on American ideals," and that he was extremely proud of the Peace Corps and the Alliance for Progress. Though the Alliance was met with some skepticism, Kennedy hoped to prove the naysayers wrong in the future.

On April 12, 1961, less than three months after Kennedy moved into the White House, the United States' greatest rival won the first round of the space race and gave the President a new priority. Soviet cosmonaut Yuri Gagarin became the first man in space when his spacecraft Vostok successfully left the Earth's atmosphere. In a 108-minute flight, Gagarin completed a full orbit of the planet. Americans were blindsided by the news. People report-ed feeling shocked and ashamed, afraid of the con-sequences of the Soviet Union's apparent scientific prowess, frustrated that they had been outdone, and even outraged. Kennedy fully grasped the impor-tance of the space race in the contest to win over the hearts and minds of Americans. He threw his support wholeheartedly behind NASA and the effort to catch up with the Soviets.

Even after being told that the cost would be ridicu-lously high and that the scientific benefit of reaching space would not be remotely on a par with the financial commitment needed, Kennedy remained adamant. He believed the space race was as important as containing the spread of Soviet influence in the effort to curb the spread of communism. Suddenly the drive to put a man in space was a matter of national security, and Kennedy once again gambled on his favorite medium. He insisted that the launches be televised.

On May 5, 1961, millions of Americans sat glued to their television sets to watch Alan Shepard attempt to become the first American in space. John and Jackie Kennedy held their breath, knowing that a success in space would take away the stress of mounting global pressures. And Shepard did it. He spent a mere 15 minutes in space, but returned safely, unharmed, and triumphant. His successful mission put the U.S. back in the space race and renewed Americans' bragging rights. Almost three weeks later Kennedy boldly spoke of the need to stay on top in the race toward new scientific achievements. "I believe this nation should commit itself to achieving the goal, before this decade is out, of landing a man on the moon and returning him safely to Earth," he declared, arguing that "no single space project in this period will be more impressive to mankind."

Not all of Kennedy's ambitious plans worked out as well. Mostly notably, in his first few months in office there was the United States' embarrassing meddling in Cuba. The Bay of Pigs invasion, a group of American-backed Cuban exiles, would attempt to take on Fidel Castro's government in hopes of igniting a civil war and toppling the leftist leader. After his election victory but prior to his Inauguration, Kennedy was briefed on the

THE FIRST LADY GREETS MEMBERS OF THE ROYAL CANADIAN NATIONAL GUARD DURING THE STATE VISIT IN MAY 1961.

specifics of the CIA-engineered plan by outgoing President Eisenhower. During the campaign, he had roundly criticized the Eisenhower Administration for allowing a "communist menace" to crop up in America's backyard, and now he inherited the problem of what to do about it. Fearing that Cuba's deepening ties to the Soviet Union could eventually put the country in harm's way, yet mindful that the U.S. should not get entangled in a war over the island nation, Kennedy nixed previously promised air support, critical to the success of the invasion, and ordered the U.S. Navy to maintain its distance.

The predawn raid on April 17, 1961, was an unmitigated disaster. Of the nearly 1,500 Cuban refugees who made it ashore, 114 were killed. The rest surrendered or were captured within two days. The new President was crushed. Not only had he sent young men to their slaughter, he had solidified Castro's position at home and strengthened the relationship between the Soviet Union and Cuba. To critics, Kennedy had humiliated the nation and confirmed the charges that he was too weak and inexperienced to deal with matters of state and international relations. Kennedy again went before the television cameras, taking full responsibility for the failure. "There's an old saying," the President said, "that victory has a hundred fathers and defeat is an orphan … I am the responsible officer of the government and that is quite obvious." In a characteristic twist of irony, just after the disaster in the Bay of Pigs, Kennedy's approval rating soared to 82 percent.

Partly in an effort to save face after the Bay of Pigs debacle, Kennedy made several important trips during his first year as President. In May 1961, the Kennedys prepared for their first official foreign trip—to Canada. Before they left, the Canadian ambassador met with White House social secretary Letitia Baldrige and warned her that they shouldn't expect a terrifically warm reception. He explained that the Canadian people were not as demonstrative and excitable as Americans and even went so far as to say that the Queen Mother had been put off by the lack of an emotional response on her own visit to Canada. Little did he know what would await Jackie when she arrived in a cleverly chosen maple leaf red suit. Huge crowds of fans camped out along the motorcade route, where shouts of "Jack-ie! Jack-ie!" could be heard over the cheers. Even their hosts were shocked.

The next month, the Kennedys flew to Paris to meet with French President Charles de Gaulle, where they showed the European establishment a new kind of American President. Kennedy impressed the aging French leader, replacing Eisenhower's military-style curtness with suave star power to great

THE KENNEDYS VISIT TO PARIS IN JUNE OF 1961 WAS FRONT-PAGE NEWS IN FRANCE.

effect. Over the course of five meetings, the two leaders discussed the situations in Berlin, Laos, and Angola, their differing opinions on NATO, and the tenuous relationship with the Soviet Union. Kennedy did his best to assure de Gaulle that he was so close an ally that an attack in Europe would be considered an attack on the United States, and that he would be willing to use nuclear weapons to ensure the safety of his European friends.

But Jackie was the real star. Prior to this trip, she had appeared on French television, and in her interview she spoke the language fluently. She had, after all, studied at the Sorbonne, spent summers in France as a child, and even preferred the French pronunciation of her name. By the time of the meeting, the French public had already heard the glamorous First Lady gush, "I was in France as a child, as a tourist, as a student, and now I am going with my husband on an official visit. I love France." And with that, she was a hit.

The French president met the Kennedys at the airport. As they drove into the city, Parisians lined the streets along the route. They cheered the motorcade and stole glances at America's new first couple. In those few days, the French public developed a taste for pillbox hats and came out squarely for Jackie, whose cosmopolitan manner, seamless language skills, and style fit in perfectly. By the time he arrived for a lunch with the French press several days into their trip, the President introduced himself simply as "the man who accompanied Jacqueline Kennedy to Paris."

At a luncheon on their first day in France, Jackie translated for her husband and for President de Gaulle. She chatted with de Gaulle in his native tongue and spoke with ease about Louis XVI, the Duc d'Angoulême, and the Bourbon dynasty, which earned her the clear respect and admiration of the politician. Before lunch was through, de Gaulle remarked to the President that Jackie knew more about France and its history than many French people. In their travels abroad, the Kennedys strove to market their American-style democracy—and largely because of Jackie's charm and aplomb, these early trips to Canada and Paris smacked of success.

After their triumph in Paris, Jack and Jackie headed to Vienna for a meeting with Soviet Premier Nikita Khrushchev. At this critical summit, Kennedy would be judged on how he stood up to the Soviet leader. During the Cold War, the game of superpower versus superpower, democracy versus communism, was being played for high stakes, and with the potential for disastrous outcomes. Image was crucial—not only in how the public perceived the two world leaders, but in how the two men perceived one another. Despite his gruff behavior and serial threats, Khrushchev was impressed with Kennedy's candor and charmed by Jackie. After their meeting, Khrushchev remarked that he liked Jackie "very much" noting that she was "youthful, energetic, and pleasant." "She knew how to make jokes," he raved, "and was, as people say, quick with her tongue." Khrushchev felt that one should be careful when speaking to her as "she has no trouble finding the right word to cut you short if you weren't." Along with the intelligence that shone through even in making small talk, her appearance and quick wit left an impression on him.

But despite Khrushchev's approval of Jackie, he attacked the President, accusing him of doing little to further the friendship between the United States and Soviet Union. Khrushchev challenged the United States' position on Berlin, and predicted that communism would ultimately triumph over capitalism. Depressed by Khrushchev's bullying, Kennedy left the summit thinking that the differences between the two superpowers would eventually lead to a nuclear confrontation. After the difficulty in Vienna, Kennedy retired to London to meet with Prime Minister Harold Macmillan. He recounted much of the Khrushchev conversation to him, and, despite their great age difference, the two statesmen found themselves easy allies, with a natural rapport that made them friends as well.

Upon their return one of Kennedy's advisers, Clark Clifford, congratulated the First Lady on her expertly played roll as an ambassador of the New Frontier. He thanked her for the most magnificent service she was doing for her country and effused, "once in a great while an individual will capture the imagination of people all over the world. You have done this; and what is more important, through your graciousness and tact, you have transformed this rare accomplishment into an incredibly important asset to this nation." As Clifford aptly wrote, the international love affair with Jackie was by no means reserved for the heads of state who dined with her. She inspired men and women in all walks of life. When Jackie visited Mexico, people in the crowd waved signs reading "Jacki si, Kennedy no," and cried "Viva Kennedy" whenever she passed. In 1962, she would undertake an extraordinary four-week journey to India where her role as goodwill ambassador was sealed.

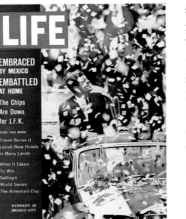

THE COVER OF *LIFE* IN JULY 1962 CELEBRATED THE KENNEDYS' WARM WELCOME IN MEXICO.

Shortly before John Kennedy decided to run for President, his father had bragged, "Jack is the greatest attraction in the country today." Hammering the thought home, Joe shared, "I'll tell you how to sell more copies of a book. Put his picture on the cover. Why is it that when his picture is on the cover of *Life* or *Redbook* they sell a record number of copies? You advertise the fact that he will be at a dinner and you will break all records for attendance. He can draw more people to a fund-raising dinner than Cary Grant or Jimmy Stewart. Why is that? He has universal appeal." And Joe was right. Men wanted to be him and women wanted to be with him. And the photographs that appeared in *Life* or *Redbook* and the other magazines sold his well-managed image to the public. And for Jackie, the same was true in spades. With her charm and grace she and her powerful husband projected an image of America that the world was eager to embrace.

THE TORCH
IS PASSED

A fresh layer of snow blanketed Washington on the bright and cold morning of Inauguration Day, January 20, 1961. Kennedy had labored long hours over his Inauguration speech, desiring that it set the right tone for his new administration. By inviting poets, writers, and artists to the festivities, he made a statement: Culture and an appreciation for the arts would characterize this Presidency. If the words of his speech did not inspire, the images did: the youngest incoming President striding beside the oldest outgoing President; the youthfulness of the President and his family. It was not hard to believe that America was truly entering a new era.

ROBERT DALLEK: Most Inaugural speeches have been forgettable cheerleading exercises. A handful, however—Jefferson's first, Lincoln's second, FDR's first, and Kennedy's—have established themselves as memorable appeals to enduring national concerns. Kennedy's address was not only beautifully written but contained language that people quote to this day: "Ask not what your country can do for you—ask what you can do for your country." The speech and Kennedy's eloquent delivery set a tone of hope for Americans—hope that the United States would once more rise to the international and domestic challenges threatening to undermine its future as a great nation. The speech gave Kennedy's administration the momentum for unprecedented achievements—such as putting a man on the moon by the end of the sixties.

LEFT: *December 1960. President Dwight D. Eisenhower greets President-elect John F. Kennedy.*
ABOVE: *January 20, 1961. President Kennedy delivers his Inaugural Address.*

ABOVE: *Thousands of well-wishers gathered at the National Guard Armory, site of the largest Inaugural Ball.*
RIGHT: *January 20, 1961. Illuminated by an ethereal glow, the new President gestures to a supporter from the presidential box overlooking the Inaugural Ball.*
PREVIOUS PAGES: *Rose Kennedy, Jacqueline Kennedy, and Richard Nixon look on as Kennedy takes the oath of office.*

BARBARA BAKER BURROWS: There is a "you are there" quality to Paul Schutzer's joyous picture of the biggest of the five Inaugural Balls, and some have come to see the message: "This way to Camelot." Paul's wife, Bernice, remembers that he considered the picture "the culmination of the entire feeling of the campaign." Paul is in the President's box just as he had been "in" the campaign for *Life*—along the way he had been mistaken for a Kennedy and babies had been pressed into his arms, and the real Kennedy had even borrowed his suits. *Life* was essential to the candidate, and the magazine had the stature and ability to commit enormous resources to the story. Today, where no media outlet so dominates, there are few who are either so essential or can afford the commitment—where trust is earned and reciprocated and whose reward is to give the reader a front row seat.

A NEW FRONTIER

The phrase "New Frontier" was a political slogan designed to shape the presidential race of 1960. But when Kennedy's staff took office the name stuck; they were an assembly of the "best and brightest" America had to offer. One key member of the new administration, Harvard professor Arthur Schlesinger, would later write of these extraordinary days, "Telephones rang incessantly. Meetings were continuous. The evenings were lively and full. The glow of the White House was lighting up the whole city ... it was a golden interlude."

ABOVE: *The "New Frontier" included (l to r) Hy Raskin, Pierre Salinger, Sargent Shriver, Larry O'Brien, John Bailey, and (seated) Ken O'Donnell, Steve Smith, and Robert Kennedy.*
RIGHT: *President Kennedy meets with senior staff during the first 100 days in office.*

LETITIA BALDRIGE: On Inauguration Day I was in the White House and saw the atmosphere change demonstrably between 11:55 a.m. and 12 noon, when the powers of government passed into the new President's hands. It was as though a beneficent tornado suddenly swept through the building, emptying the house of its former pace and old flavors, and injecting a new life, and extremely hyperactive tempo, and a sheer unadulterated joy that seemed to burst from its new occupants. Staffers went around embracing one another—"I can't believe it! We're here! We're actually here!"

HUGH SIDEY: Flooding in from all corners of the nation, but particularly from Kennedy's New England, were the former GIs who had fought the war and gone to college in unprecedented numbers and hurried to Washington with their idealism on their sleeves—yes, there would be a New Frontier. Something called the "Irish Mafia" took up White House staff niches; Harvard professors like Arthur Schlesinger, Jr., moved in. Bobby Kennedy's Virginia estate, Hickory Hill, became a locus of power and play for this new and elegantly tailored society. A new age had arrived.

ABOVE: *March 21, 1963. JFK departs the State Department briefing room following a press conference.*
RIGHT: *February 2, 1963. President Kennedy calls on a member of the press.*

HUGH SIDEY: Kennedy's televised press conferences were dubbed "the best matinee" in Washington. There was very little debate about how wise it was to expose the President in this manner. Kennedy brushed it aside, fully aware that from his experience and expansive reading he was in most cases better informed on most issues than any of the questioners. Got a question on shipping? He could quote from a recent study. Khrushchev's "wars of liberation" speech? He knew the disturbing parts. Always armed with humor, he ruled the stage and exited with his audience wanting more.

ROBERT DALLEK: Kennedy's televised press conferences helped solidify his hold on the country. His intelligence, wit, charm, and substantive command convinced journalists and a larger public that he was worthy of the Presidency. He became a familiar chief executive who did not hide behind administration spokesmen, but a leader who spoke directly to the people and cultivated their support in addressing domestic and foreign crises.

HUGH SIDEY: By Kennedy's reckoning there were legions of young people who would like to serve their country in some capacity but had neither the connections nor the money to maneuver for political office. Aware that his Navy service was one of the best experiences in his life, he calculated that a civilian service corps would respond enthusiastically to a call to give some time from their young lives to help those in need around the globe. He was right about the mood of the nation's young. He raised the challenge and hundreds of thousands of Americans enrolled to work under his banner. And the Kennedy legend grew, not only in West Virginia but in India and around the world.

ROBERT DALLEK: Kennedy's introduction of the Peace Corps gave substance to his appeal for sacrifice on the part of Americans. As important, it asked younger Americans to join him not in taking up arms against communism and other forms of political repression, but in fighting for "the hearts and minds" of peoples in developing nations tempted by command economies and authoritarian governments promising radical solutions to seemingly insoluble problems.

LEFT: *November 1, 1961. Some of the first Peace Corps volunteers listen to village children read in Colombia.*
BELOW: *August 1962. President Kennedy greets Peace Corps volunteers on the White House lawn.*

SPACE RACE

Less than a month after Alan Shepard made his historic 15-minute flight on May 5, 1961, becoming the first American in space, President Kennedy announced an ambitious goal during a speech to Congress on urgent national needs: to land an astronaut on the moon before the end of the decade. This was the boldest move yet in the ongoing space race between the Soviet Union and the United States, and it was, until then, a possibility that had existed only in science fiction. Kennedy's charge ignited the public's imagination. Huge audiences tuned in to watch John Glenn's February 20, 1962, orbital flight. The astronaut received a hero's welcome—and a Distinguished Service Medal from the President.

ABOVE: *February 23, 1962. President Kennedy and John Glenn inspect the interior of Friendship 7.*
RIGHT: *May 5, 1961. John and Jacqueline Kennedy watch Alan Shepard's historic flight.*

LETITIA BALDRIGE: The Kennedys were like children in their excitement about the success of America's space program. When John Glenn came to the Rose Garden after his sensational trip to outer space, his helicopter arrived ahead of schedule (something that is not supposed to happen at the White House). As a result, the most important figures in the U.S. government and the entire diplomatic corps were seen running up the South Lawn—and panting heavily—so that they wouldn't miss honoring the man who was America's greatest hero at the moment.

BARBARA BAKER BURROWS: It would be very difficult to re-create the public excitement that accompanied the space program throughout the 1960s. In a way that is unfathomable now, but attests to the power of *Life* then, the magazine acquired exclusive rights to cover the U.S. space program. It was a heady time for *Life* and its readers, for the administration, and for the exploration of space—what could better symbolize a new frontier?

HUGH SIDEY: The way the images of the Kennedys at work and in vigorous play flow together, it would be easy to suggest that there was a scriptwriter backstage arranging events and costumes, not an unknown approach then and now in politics. But in the case of the Kennedys, most of the action was natural, though there was no question that it could and would be tweaked for maximum national appeal. There was just something in the Kennedy brain which automatically sensed appealing imagery. Let it roll—with a gentle shove or two. John Kennedy had played an enthusiastic game of touch football. He had been a devoted captain of his small sailboats. His ailing back had crimped his indulgence, but with a public that relished the idea of Kennedy "viggaa," he did whatever he could to keep the idea alive that he was still a competitor, in one way or another. He played a few rounds of golf when he was at Hyannis Port or Hammersmith Farm. It was not intensive golf, and cameras were shooed away after the first tee, which of course showed a fluid swing and led to speculation that he could be a scratch golfer if he ever had the time. Back in the campaign, when it was suggested he get a warmer overcoat for Wisconsin chills, he declined, explaining he had always worn a dress overcoat and would not alter the image of the disciplined young Brahmin. In this picture, Kennedy, with his usual humor, has removed his sport coat, loosened his tie and stands nonchalantly in the cold wind from Narragansett Bay. Pierre Salinger, his press secretary, was never what you could call a "fall guy." But Pierre was not a rugged outdoorsman, preferring cozy bistros, fine wines, and big cigars. Salinger in his tightly drawn parka next to the exposed President was worth a laugh—and a photograph or two. Both men thought it all in a day's imaging.

BARBARA BAKER BURROWS: It was a really nippy September day on the deck of the U.S.S. *Joseph Kennedy, Jr.* Not quite so stormy as to require the foul weather gear sported by the urbane press secretary, Pierre Salinger, but even a hard-bitten New Englander needed a jacket. Also aboard, White House photographer Cecil Stoughton remembers being waved off by the President when he first approached with a camera. Kennedy, wanting to have some fun at Pierre's expense, started loosening his tie and unbuttoning his shirt, before giving Cecil the sign that the scene was picture perfect. Here was a President's self-made photo op. In his confident pose he managed to further enhance his image of youthful vigor, and to display the mischieviousness that could make him so endearing. Cecil remembers, too, an unusual photograph he took that afternoon, the rare scene of Jackie kneeling beside the President with her arm around his shoulder [p. 151]. Surprisingly, and not necessarily the way we remember it, they were careful about being too demonstrative in public. For Cecil, perhaps the happiest memory of that day is the picture in his mind of his son and young Caroline, with Kennedy's encouragement, chasing each other around the ship. The fun did not necessarily end when the formal picture taking was done.

LEFT: *September 22, 1962. President Kennedy and Pierre Salinger on the deck of the U.S.S.* Joseph Kennedy, Jr., *during the America's Cup race in Newport, Rhode Island.*

CASTING IMAGES ABROAD

Making their first trips abroad in the spring of 1961, the Kennedys were greeted with unexpected warmth in Canada in May. Jubilant crowds chanted "Jack-ie, Jack-ie," charmed by her speaking French and her bright red suit, which echoed the bright red maple leaf of Canada's flag. But no one anticipated what would happen in France and then Vienna later that spring: Thousands crowded for a glimpse of the young American President and his beautiful wife. Jackie's knowledge of French history impressed French President Charles de Gaulle, and her Bouvier ancestry and admiration of French fashion and culture drew the enthusiasm of thousands. Although the President's Vienna summit just days later fell short of his expectation, it was nevertheless becoming clear that the Kennedys were broadcasting an image of America that the world was eager to embrace.

LEFT: *May 31, 1961. Dressed in an elegant lace sheath, Jackie attends a white-tie reception at the Elysée Palace.*
ABOVE: *June 2, 1961. In the shadow of the Eiffel Tower, JFK enters the Palais de Chaillot for a NATO address.*

LETITIA BALDRIGE: The French were ecstatic over Jackie's trip to France. None of us will ever forget the reception Jackie received as her car, with or without the President, moved through the streets of Paris. The chant "Jack-ie, Jack-ie" became a familiar one. Here was an American, speaking French and dressed in French haute couture, knowledgeable about French history and art. To the French people she was one of them. "Vive Jackie!" was heard everywhere. She had taken on a kind of power of her own.

HUGH SIDEY: I remember when Kennedy landed in Paris the clouds parted and the sun came out—which is just amazing. We called it "the Kennedy Luck." De Gaulle was very much down on the United States, and it promised to be a tough exchange. But then Jack gave a very gracious speech. And then Jackie spoke in French. They looked so good. And they talked so well. You could see old de Gaulle beginning to melt right then. As an American citizen I was profoundly proud of these young people, and I think that was reflected all over the country.

LETITIA BALDRIGE: President de Gaulle (seated on Jackie's right), and Madame de Gaulle (seated on President Kennedy's right) gave the farewell dinner of dinners for their honored guests from the United States on the last night of their visit. It was held in Louis XV's Hall of Mirrors at Versailles. Jackie wore a magnificent ball gown from Givenchy of ivory satin embroidered with sequined flowers. The table stretched almost the length of the gallery, one wall of which was all windows, while the opposite one was lined in mirrors, set into giant hand-carved frames, an 18th-century "first" in interior design. Except for the newly illuminated ceiling frescoes, there was only candlelight, bathing the table in a golden glow, which was then reflected back from the mirrors onto the vermeil silver-gilt candelabra and table appointments. The air was fragrant with thousands of flowers that discreetly decorated the table. The guests had no dilemma about what to wear this night. The men were in white tie and tails, wearing their decorations. The women were in ball gowns, elbow-length white gloves, and serious jewels. If they didn't own them, the jewelers were more than happy to lend them anything. This was the biggest night in Paris since before the war.

Nothing was overdone, even if it was the most opulent scene possible. (I could see Jackie secretly comparing this venue for a state dinner with the one she oversaw in the White House.) After dinner a ballet, commissioned by Louis XV, was performed in the newly restored pale blue, ivory, and gold theater at one end of the palace. The dancers wore costumes of the period, and danced to music of the period. There were torch-footlights on the stage. Afterward, the cortege of cars left to return to Paris, driving through its illuminated forest, with giant fountains splashing diamond sparkles in the light, and with the two countries' national anthems playing mysteriously through loudspeakers in the trees. It was magical, unforgettable!

PREVIOUS PAGES: *June 1, 1961. The Kennedys attend a banquet dinner in the Palace of Versailles's famed Hall of Mirrors.*

ABOVE: June 2, 1961. Soviet Premier Nikita Khrushchev and John Kennedy meet for the first time in Vienna, Austria.
RIGHT: June 4, 1961. Kennedy and press secretary Pierre Salinger discuss bad press over the Vienna talks.

HUGH SIDEY: Kennedy was shocked by Khrushchev's responses and actions in Vienna. Through all of his political life, Kennedy had said when there was a problem that had to be solved for the good of the people that political adversaries could sit down and say OK, we have got to quit arguing about this. We have got to solve it for everyone's good. And he had always reached an accommodation. But he sat with Khrushchev and said we just can't let a nuclear exchange take place. Seventy million people will be killed in the first ten minutes. And Khrushchev didn't answer—as if to say the deaths of 70 million people didn't matter.

ROBERT DALLEK: Kennedy viewed the meeting in Vienna with Khrushchev as something of a disaster. He told *New York Times* columnist James Reston that it was the "roughest thing in my life." Instead of easing Soviet-American tensions over Berlin, it seemed to exacerbate them. To combat Khrushchev's impressions of a young man who had faltered in the Bay of Pigs crisis and failed to stand up to him in Vienna, Kennedy felt compelled to call up military reserves as a demonstration that he was ready to fight to preserve U.S. rights in Berlin.

ABOVE: *December 16, 1961. Jacqueline Kennedy addresses the crowd at La Morita, Venezuela, in Spanish.*
RIGHT: *November 5, 1962. The Kennedys are welcomed by a ticker tape parade in Rio de Janeiro.*
FOLLOWING PAGES: *December 1961. Jackie Kennedy waves good-bye to a patient in a Bogotá, Colombia, pediatric ward.*

ROBERT DALLEK: Kennedy understood that the rest of the world looked to the United States for leadership. And that the U.S. was vitally connected to matters everywhere—that it could not ignore what was going on in Europe or the Middle East or Africa or Latin America. In a sense he was a world statesman. And the world responded to this. This was the new America—the America that could resolve differences in the Cold War and assure peace. Kennedy became a great hero not only to Americans but to people all over the globe. I am told that to this day you can still go into homes in Africa and Latin America and see photos of John Kennedy on the walls.

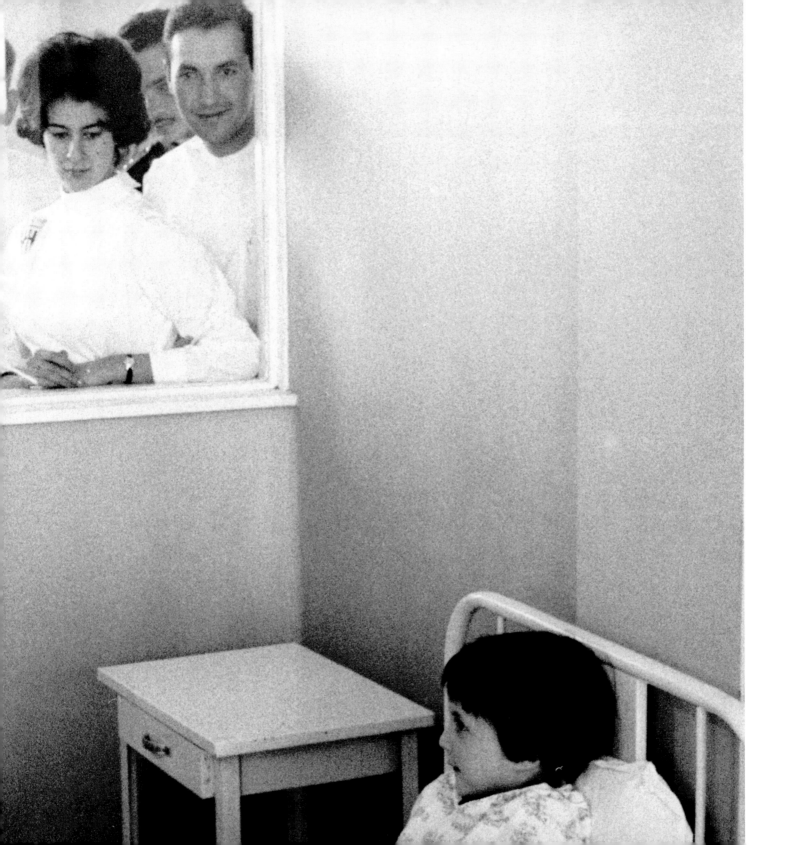

JACKIE: A GOODWILL AMBASSADOR

Jackie's tremendous appeal abroad led to an official state visit to India and Pakistan in early 1962. Her trip began with a special audience with the pope in Italy, and then continued on to India and Pakistan. A gaggle of reporters followed, commenting on every aspect of the First Lady's wardrobe, which featured vibrant colors that echoed hues of the countries she visited. Through her grace and appreciative sensitivity to the sights and experiences, the First Lady projected an image of America as youthful and interested in other cultures. A documentary film about the trip aired all over the world. Jackie was proving to be as powerful a political force as her husband.

BELOW: *March 11, 1962. Jackie attends an audience with the pope.*
RIGHT: *March 17, 1962. The First Lady attends an official function in Udaipur, India.*

LETITIA BALDRIGE: Jackie, accompanied by her sister Lee Radziwill, made a masterfully produced "state" visit on behalf of the United States to Prime Minister Nehru in India and to Gen. Ayub Khan in Pakistan. It was a first for the United States government to use a First Lady as its representative to another government, but it set a precedent that has been followed ever since.

In India, Jackie and Lee rode atop a camel and an elephant, watched a cobra fight a mongoose at teatime in the prime minister's garden, stood stunned by the beauty of the Taj Mahal, watched the making of colorful saris, toured all of the great moghul art museums and galleries, and "beavered through" enough state banquets to last them a century. They were followed by crowds wherever they went, and what amazed the staff accompanying the First Lady was the number of photographs of her with the President, or of her alone, with burning votive lights in front of them, which had been mounted on the walls of the caves where poor people lived in Delhi.

The brilliance of the colors in India, the pungent odors, the people everywhere—day and night—the people, the people—left a permanent impression on everyone involved in this diplomatic journey. Who could have predicted back in 1961 that Pakistan would become the center of our involvement in fighting the Middle East terrorists close to half a century later? Who could have foretold that India, a backward country at the time of Mrs. Kennedy's visit, would become such a thriving international business center? Jackie's trip may have put the United States on the map for Indians, but it also put India on the map for Americans.

BARBARA BAKER BURROWS: When Jackie traveled abroad, she was a sensation, captivating the hearts of the public and leaders alike. Never topped was her reception in Paris. "Hell," exulted Kennedy aide Dave Powers. "They couldn't get this kind of turnout for the Second Coming." Jackie spoke French (and Italian and Spanish), had studied European history, and knew art. She was interested in everything. Here was a new kind of American, a glamorous one at that, and a cartoonist pictured a smitten French President de Gaulle in bed with his wife, but dreaming of Jackie. Finally, it fell to her husband to introduce himself as the man who accompanied Jacqueline Kennedy to Paris to complete the coronation.

First ladies hadn't traveled extensively, and certainly not with this level of excitement and success. From Vienna, where Khrushchev flirted with Jackie, to Colombia, where she astonished people by kissing sick children in an orphanage, the world had seen nothing like her. Her visits to India and Pakistan were diplomatic triumphs. Nehru showered her with gifts, and she, in turn, showed her passion for Indian culture. So taken was Jackie by the soft morning light at the Taj Mahal that she returned to stand before it in the moonlight. And when she asked to partake in the celebration of Holi, the Secret Service advised against her taking part in the festival which involved throwing a powder of colored chalk. "They said the powder was made from manure. I said I didn't care, and I did it anyway." She left India known as "*Ameriki Rani—Queen of America.*"

LEFT: *March 25, 1962. The First Lady and sister Lee Radziwill ride a camel in Karachi, Pakistan.*

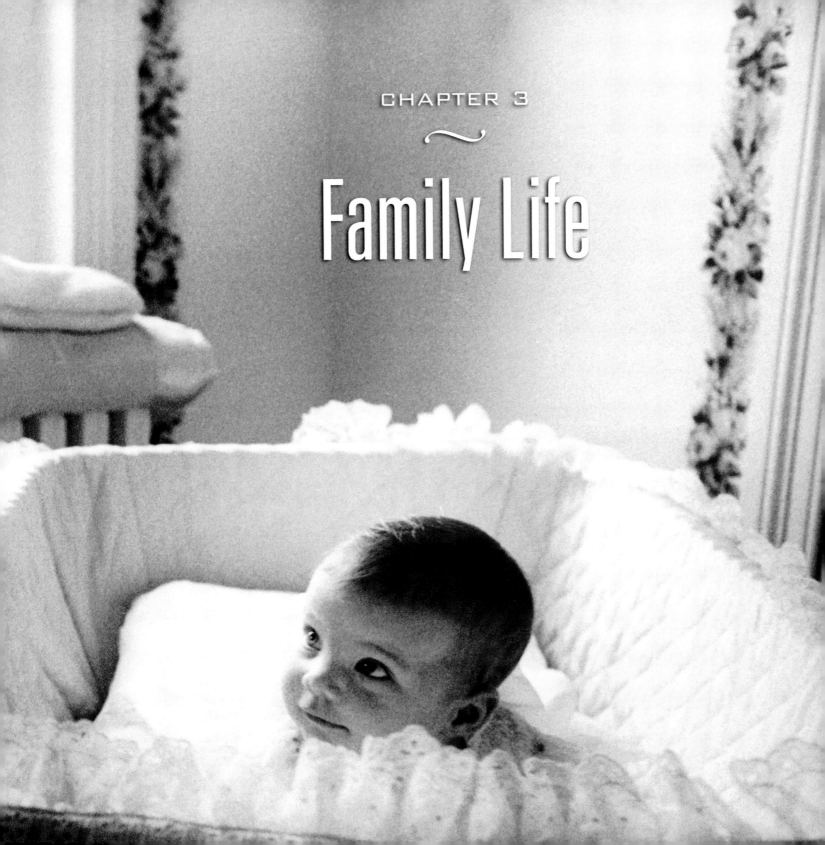

CHAPTER 3

Family Life

Shortly after their enormous, fairy-tale wedding, legendary broadcaster Edward R. Murrow interviewed Jack and Jackie Kennedy on the television program *Person to Person*. While the men bantered about social issues and foreign affairs, Jackie shyly discussed housewares. Since the President's stake in the Kennedy family fortune amounted to several hundred thousand dollars a year (the average salary in 1960 was under $5,000), and Jackie was from a well-off family as well, it is doubtful that she had ever done much in the way of housework. Nonetheless, the woman who excelled at languages, writing, and art made a special effort to present herself as a traditional, supportive spouse and the perfect political wife.

Jackie had married into a formidable family. With brothers and sisters and seemingly countless numbers of nieces and nephews focused around life in Hyannis Port, the reserved Jackie had some difficulty fitting into the boisterous, athletic Kennedy family. Observers have commented that Jackie knew what she was getting into when she married Jack Kennedy. He was, they point out, much like her father, "Black Jack" Bouvier—a consummate flirt and philanderer with a seemingly bottomless income. Whether or not she should have been prepared for Jack's independence and wandering eye, she was by all reports hugely let down after the wedding. She was shocked by the amount of time he spent with his friends. Recalling that she was alone almost every weekend, she said, "It was all wrong. Politics was sort of my enemy and we had no home life whatsoever." It is rumored that as early as 1955, Jackie was ready for a divorce.

Despite their marital troubles, John and Jackie made a good team on the campaign trail. On a crucial trip to West Virginia during the presidential primary, she charmed audiences with talk of their new family. Jackie reported that two-year-old Caroline's vocabulary was growing steadily on the campaign trail; her "first words were 'plane,' 'good-bye,' and 'New Hampshire,' and just this morning, she said 'Wisconsin,' and 'West Virginia.'" She also made concessions about her glamorous wardrobe and personal spending to silence her critics. "All the talk over what I wear and how I fix my hair has amused and puzzled me...." She said, "What does my hairdo have to do with my husband's ability to be President?" Nonetheless, she played her part well and tried to help her husband with his. As she got further along in her pregnancy with John Jr., she shied away from vigorous public campaigning, but when they moved into the White House, she did everything she could to make her husband's Presidency—and their marriage—work.

It had been many years since a family with such young, adorable children lived in the White House. In 1901, Teddy Roosevelt moved into the White House with his bustling family, and photographers could never get enough of them. In the case of the Kennedys, the pairing of a glamorous couple and two photogenic little ones captivated the country. Even before they moved into the White House, Caroline and John were subjects that sold magazines.

In December 1960, *Life* dedicated its cover and an entire page complete with six pictures to John Jr.'s baptism. Entitled "The High Point in a Notable Week," the piece juxtaposed Kennedy's important jobs: being a dad and appointing a Cabinet. But Jackie was adamant about keeping her children out of the spotlight. In an attempt to let the children lead as normal a life as possible, they set up a nursery school in the White House so

LEFT: *September 30, 1963. The Kennedy family at Camp David.*
PREVIOUS PAGES: *March 25, 1958. Four-month-old Caroline smiles at her senator father from her crib.*

that the Kennedy kids could be taught alongside children of the same ages.

The Kennedys went to great lengths to make the White House a home. Jack set up family photos on his desk, like any other husband and father might do. Caroline was delighted to learn their new house had a pool, and was bowled over by the enormous snowman that greeted her in the presidential backyard, complete with buttons for eyes and a carrot nose. Jackie was quick to release details on the children's rooms (Caroline's room was pink with white trim, John-John's white with blue trim), but she was not setting a precedent. Only reluctantly did she divulge information about her children or the family's private time in the White House. As far as she was concerned, the press would have to make do with a standard fare of released menus, state functions, and the occasional photo op.

Much of the media coverage of the first family centered around their image as ideal parents going about normal parent business: putting the children to bed, reading them stories, getting dressed for Halloween, splashing in the ocean. One of Jackie's many *Life* magazine features included a photo of the First Lady playing with Caroline and some of her cousins. After every article featuring some new minute aspect of the first family's life the letters poured in from an adoring public. People from every state in the Union wanted to know what the children ate and what time they went to bed. One letter read: "If I could be one-half as good a mother to my children as you are to yours...."

THE ENTIRE KENNEDY CLAN IS PICTURED ON THE BEACH IN HYANNIS PORT IN 1931.

Jack took time out of his schedule to spend with his children, and whatever his shortcomings as a husband, he did love them mightily. Unlike Jackie, though, he did not see why his love for them and his desire to use them to brighten his image had to be mutually exclusive. He enjoyed the company of photographers and newsmen and liked having them around to witness the moments he spent with his children. He knew that with the kids present there was always the possibility of a touching moment just around the corner. Jackie did occasionally agree to allow photo shoots with the children, and they resulted in some cherished images. Though the timing and circumstance of the most memorable photographs may have been contrived—how many women put their children to bed dressed in heels, pearls, and full lipstick?—they spoke volumes of encouragement to the public.

Although she preferred to stay out of politics, Jackie played her roles as mother and political wife very well. She embraced her goodwill trips and charmed world leaders when it was helpful. She toured the Parthenon with the wife of the Greek premier, lunched with the Queen at Buckingham Palace, strolled through gardens with Jawaharlal Nehru, rode a camel in Karachi, and spoke effortless Spanish throughout South America. And she remained an inspiring hostess and devoted mother despite the lonely life she married into. Members of the Secret Service have reported feeling sorry for the First Lady. One agent reported, "She was real lonesome.... She seemed sad—

just a sad lady." But she played her part with aplomb and remained stoic as she lost two children and struggled with the knowledge of her husband's infidelity.

The need to keep personal matters under lock and key upset Jackie, but she found ways to cope. In an early letter to her press secretary, Pam Turnure, Jackie wrote, "I have suddenly realized what it means to completely lose one's privacy." Right after moving into the White House, Jackie made it clear that she would like to keep to herself whenever possible. The chief of protocol met with her to discuss her role in the administration and asked her what, in addition to traditional duties, she might be interested in doing. "As little as possible," she replied. "I'm a mother. I'm a wife. I'm not a public official." In a letter to Bill Walton, who assisted her with the restoration of the White House and headed the Fine Arts Commission, she explained the coup that she pulled off. "I was tired—and I wanted to see my children—so I told Tish [Letitia Baldrige]—who nearly died from shock—that I would *never* go out—lunches, teas, degrees, speeches, etc. For two months it was a flap. Now it is a precedent established … now, my life here, which I dreaded—and which at first overwhelmed me—is now all under control and the happiest time I have ever known—not for the position—but the closeness of one's

YOUNG JACKIE BOUVIER RIDES HORSEBACK AS HER FATHER, JOHN, WALKS BY HER SIDE. UPON SEEING THIS PHOTO, HER CHIEF OF STAFF QUIPPED, "HER ATTITUDE TOWARD THE PRESS WAS APPARENT AT AN EARLY AGE."

family—the last thing I expected to find in the W. House."

The struggle to maintain a measure of privacy for herself and her children would be an ongoing one for Jackie. She was infuriated when one enterprising toy company issued "Caroline" dolls and threatened retribution. There was a play area on the grounds, and when Jackie found out that while in line for White House tours, people could see the playground, she asked that tall bushes be planted there. She also knew how to intimidate photographers, many of whom knew that the President might invite them to shoot photos at a time or place not approved by his wife. Photographer Jacques Lowe recalled a time when Jack invited him to take photos that Jackie had specifically asked him not to. After being assured by the President that the pictures were indeed wanted, he took the shots. Later, Lowe was pulled aside and berated by a very angry Jackie. The President, looking on, smiled meekly and agreed that Lowe shouldn't do that again. In this way, the President got what he needed—adorable family photos that would reassure the American people that all was well with the world—without having to argue with his wife. Stanley Tretick also remembered a particular event where the ever watchful First Lady caught his eye and said, "Oh, now, you're not here to photograph us, are you Stanley? Or Caroline either?"

Tretick said of Jackie: "Mrs. Kennedy has a way that strikes terror into your heart. She was a very strong-minded girl and tough."

At the suggestion of Maj. Gen. Chester Clifton, Kennedy's military aide, Cecil Stoughton was installed as the official White House photographer. The first photographer to hold such a position, Stoughton was given an office in the West Wing, where a bell signaled that his service was needed. Stoughton's unusual access to the Kennedy's private life greatly expanded the public's view of the presidency, and gave the Kennedys a way to manage at least a portion of their public image. As Stoughton said, "the advantage of having an in-house photographer was that they knew they could control me—if I did something wrong I'd end up in Guam the next day!"

John Jr. made the cover of *Life* again in November 1961, around the time of his first birthday, and the article that accompanied the huge, double-page photos of John and Caroline playing mentioned the rarity of such glimpses into the presidential nursery. "As befits a member in good standing of the robust Kennedy clan, he is energetic, sturdy and outgoing, with a heavy thatch of wayward brown hair. According to a recent (and rare) White House bulletin, John weighs 23 pounds, is 30 inches tall and has seven teeth, which is about average for his age."

One can only imagine what Jackie thought about having to send out a press release about her children's height and weight. And every member of the family got the star treatment. When Caroline's cat, Tom Kitten, made the transition from his temporary home at the Auchincloss estate in Virginia to the White House, even he got a full interview with pictures.

Her children were not the only things dear to Jackie that she wanted kept from photographers. She was proud of the

SHORTLY AFTER CAROLINE'S BIRTH, THE KENNEDY FAMILY APPEARED ON THE COVER OF *LIFE*.

home that she and her husband built in Virginia. "I designed it all myself," she beamed. "I don't want it to be exploited and photographed all over the place." The Virginia getaway was one of her few private havens, as the press tended to follow them everywhere, including when they sailed on the *Honey Fitz*. The press had their own boat and would remain a short distance away. With their cameras and binoculars, they would catch images of Jackie water-skiing or Caroline playing. Once, after Jackie peered back at the press boat with her own set of binoculars, a correspondent sent a note to Pierre Salinger complaining that she had invaded *their* privacy.

The President's attitude toward the press couldn't have been more different. He enjoyed their company and allowed exclusive access to journalists with whom he felt comfortable. When the *New York Times* Washington bureau chief suggested that this practice was not a good idea, Pierre Salinger reminded him that the President would speak to whomever he desired, whenever he chose. Many newsmen saw aspects of the White House for the first time during the Kennedy Administration, whether it was a glittering state reception, a glimpse of the pool, or even an invitation into the presidential quarters, and many reporters left the Kennedy White House with colorful anecdotes. Hugh Sidey once turned up for an interview and the President suggested they go for a dip in the pool. Sidey pointed out that it hadn't occurred to him to bring a bathing suit. "You don't need one" was the President's reply. They hopped into the pool and the President did the interview au natural. Not surprisingly, Jack's openness with reporters was a bone of contention with his wife, who had no interest in relinquishing any more of her privacy.

While Jackie was away, her husband took advantage of her absence and invited Stanley Tretick over to photograph the kids. The photographer recalled the President's words: "Things get kind of sticky around here when Mrs. Kennedy's around. But Mrs. Kennedy is away. So, now is the time to do some of those pictures you've been asking for of John and Caroline." His five days of shooting resulted in many of the iconic fatherly photos of the President, including the shot of John-John peaking out from underneath his father's desk. Glancing over Tretick's contact sheets, Jack picked it out of the bunch and exclaimed, "With this one, you can't lose."

The article, "The President and His Son," boasted ten pages of photos, and many of the captions were penned in John-John's young "voice." The innocent images of an inquisitive little boy further proved that the man in the White House was just like every other dad out there, who lived with a lovable little mischief-maker playing at his feet. Though shot in October, the photos did not appear in *Look* magazine until the December 3rd issue, reaching subscribers four days before John-John's third birthday and one day before the fateful events in Dallas. These photos and more reappeared in an issue soon after the assassination, entitled *Kennedy and His Family in Pictures*.

JFK NAVIGATES A GOLF CART FULL OF NIECES AND NEPHEWS IN THIS 1962 *LOOK* COVER.

In early August 1963, Jackie gave birth to a second little boy, Patrick Bouvier. The not-quite-five-pound baby had serious respiratory complications and died within three days of his premature birth. Both parents were devastated. And the country joined in their pain, flooding the White House with their condolences. Americans from coast to coast could identify with their loss. That the most powerful couple in the world would be forced to endure such a hardship only made them more human, more accessible.

At a period in history when fears of communism and social strife kept the populace tense, portrayals of the White House as a home rather than a command center were calming. The situation abroad couldn't be too dire if the Kennedys were still hosting dinner parties and playing with their kids. One aspect of the new Kennedy style of entertaining recalled "normal" couples entertaining—they wanted their guests to feel comfortable and to enjoy the evenings. Liquor was served instead of just punch, and ashtrays were put out for the guests. Fireplaces were unblocked to keep guests warm and comfortable. A startled society columnist who attended an early function listed numerous White House social norms that had been broken. She wrote, "President and Mrs. Kennedy have decided that they are going to offer the same hospitality to their guests when reporters are present as they would naturally do if they weren't, or if they were living back in their own house on N Street."

Any attempt to characterize the Kennedys as normal would be a silly one—they were far too wealthy a couple to identify with the average household. They owned getaways in Hyannis Port and Palm Beach, had their own plane, employed a clothing designer and French chef, frequently traveled without one another, and counted royalty and celebrities among their close family ties. But while they lived very different lives than the average American citizen, the images in the media emphasized the traits that anyone could identify with and helped inculcate in the public feelings of trust and camaraderie. In the Kennedy family America found its best image of itself: young, smiling, rich, and happy. These images spawned a fascination that still surges today, with the public eager for the next book of Kennedy family revelations—or even rarer—an unseen family photograph. Through a perfect combination of traits, the Kennedys fulfilled an ideal of America at a unique time in history, creating an enduring myth that remains, decades later, unshakable.

EXTENDED FAMILY

With a family of nine children, there were plenty of Kennedys to assist with all aspects of running for office, from the tea parties thrown by the Kennedy women to Bobby's well-organized management of his brother's campaign. On the campaign trail, younger brother Ted lent a hand, as did movie-star brother-in-law Peter Lawford, who used his Hollywood connections to help build support for Kennedy's campaign. Sargent Shriver, husband of sister Eunice, pitched in too. That they were all young, wealthy, and good-looking only added to the aura that followed Kennedy. The locus of family operations was Joe Kennedy's Hyannis Port home. It was here that the family would gather to hear the results of the 1960 presidential race.

LEFT: *July 1960. John and his brother and campaign organizer Bobby Kennedy confer in their Los Angeles hotel suite.*
ABOVE: *Family members (l-r) Eunice Shriver, Ethel Kennedy, Peter Lawford, and Joan Kennedy in Hyannis Port on election night.*

LETITIA BALDRIGE: The Kennedys needed no friends—they were an entire conclave unto themselves. They constantly got together, moving, as one wag described it, in elephant hordes. Father Joe saw to it they talked politics more than gossip. If anyone was having a problem, it was up to the entire family to work on the problem. It was an atmosphere of fun, a lot of kidding around, and yet also of a serious seeking of goals, a sense of duty, the guarantee of family support, and the respect for public office.

ROBERT DALLEK: Joe Kennedy believed that for his sons, John, Bobby, and Ted, to succeed in politics, they needed to rely on each other rather than outside advisers. The three brothers embraced Joe's advice and put family ties at the center of their political actions. Jack made Bobby his attorney general and encouraged Ted to run for the Senate from Massachusetts. Bobby was Jack's closest confidant and the most trusted member of his administration.

LEFT: *July 7, 1953. Jackie plays touch football with members of the Kennedy clan on a huge lawn of the Kennedys' summer house.*
ABOVE: *Photo-booth snapshot of John and Jackie, ca 1953.*

HUGH SIDEY: Like many parts of the Kennedy legend, athletic competition was spawned naturally within a rambunctious young clan and their friends. As the Kennedys accumulated power and fame, the clashes on the friendly fields of play became the stuff of literature. Senators, Cabinet officers, judges, and authors were swept into the rowdy games whether they liked it or not. Not all of them did, nor did Jackie, who made no secret of the fact she often was not in the mood for the rough and tumble, instead preferring to curl up with a good book. Family patriarch Joe Kennedy planned it that way, once explaining he wanted give and take at the dinner table on important national issues, and he wanted physical exertion in the yard with touch football, tennis, and sailing. He said he bought his home in Hyannis Port because the front yard leading to the dock was a natural, level field for the football skirmishes.

DAWN OF CAMELOT

Jacqueline Bouvier's marriage to Jack Kennedy in 1953 brought her fully into the Kennedy circle. Not used to the political life, she declared in an early interview that she preferred housekeeping to politics. Her grace and appreciation of culture proved a disarming complement to Jack's rugged athletic persona. After several years of living with both sets of parents the couple settled into a Georgetown town house. In 1957, daughter Caroline was born, completing the picture of the happy young family.

ABOVE: *September 12, 1953. John and Jackie pose with their bridesmaids, groomsmen, and ushers on their wedding day.*
RIGHT: *Jacqueline Kennedy at Merrywood, her mother's home in Virginia, 1959*

BARBARA BAKER BURROWS: To the Kennedy family's ample quotient of glamour, Jackie brought even more. With it, she seemed to temper the brashness of their ambition, providing a finishing school touch to ready its chosen candidate for high office. Her interests were art and literature and language, not politics. She also brought her own family: wealthy stepfather, an elegant sister, a brother-in-law prince, and even a touch of intrigue in her kept-from-view father "Black Jack" Bouvier. Together, the families brought an army of ambassadors to the campaign trail, but Kennedy aide Dave Powers claimed that just having Jackie along could double the size of a crowd.

LETITIA BALDRIGE: At the beginning of their marriage, Jackie tried hard to fit in with the athletic side of the Kennedy family. It was a necessity, not a matter of choice when you married a Kennedy. But she soon tired of touch football and of all the physical horsing around and managed very deftly to absent herself from it.

BARBARA BAKER BURROWS: It would be hard to exaggerate the reach and power of the weekly *Life* in its prime. Photographers wanted to shoot for it, and their subjects sought to be in it—a combination that gave the magazine unmatched access. Here was the pinnacle of photography, where a subject could expect to be treated fairly, in a mass market publication. *Life* had, of course, chronicled the Kennedys, but then Jackie came along. They gave her the cover, the first national magazine to do so. And then they did it another 17 times. No one had more; only her husband came close. Whether to cover Jack and Jackie was not a difficult editorial decision. It may not even have required great photographers, but that's who *Life* brought to the assignment. In addition to Paul Schutzer, Mark Shaw, and Jacques Lowe, the pictures of Hank Walker, Hy Peskin, Yale Joel, Alfred Eisenstaedt, Art Rickerby, and Ed Clark filled the magazine's pages. There were many others, and the intimacy of the long association continued notably with Bill Eppridge through Bobby's campaigns and to his death in Los Angeles. For Jackie, too; her last business appointment, six weeks before her death, was with *Life*.

LEFT: *May 1959. The Senator says good-bye in the doorway of the couple's Georgetown home.*
BELOW: *Caroline and Jackie splash in a backyard pool, 1959.*

READY TO RUN

In the summers of 1959 and 1960, photographers Mark Shaw and Jacques Lowe among others captured images of the Kennedys vacationing at their Hyannis Port home. Relaxed photographs of Jack Kennedy on the beach, romping with his beautiful wife and daughter, introduced a handsome young family to America and helped to position the candidate as he began his presidential race.

ABOVE: *Summer 1960. John, Caroline, and Jackie pause for a family snapshot in this Jacques Lowe photo.*
LEFT: *John F. Kennedy hoists Caroline into the air on the beach in Hyannis Port in this classic Mark Shaw image.*
FOLLOWING PAGES: *Summer 1959. Life photographer Mark Shaw caught Jackie swinging a delighted Caroline over the water in Nantucket Sound.*

ROBERT DALLEK: Kennedy's image as a family man was part of the public relations that attracted Americans to Kennedy. The children, Caroline and John-John, were a tremendous political asset. Jacqueline Kennedy was an extraordinary political asset because she was so beautiful, so aristocratic. She gave Americans the feeling that they would have an aristocrat in the White House.

BARBARA BAKER BURROWS: From a first meeting on assignment for *Life* during the 1959 campaign, Mark Shaw became the Kennedys' unofficial family photographer. It's in those family pictures, particularly those of the children, that so much of the parents is revealed. Mark did try to remain unobtrusive, preferring to work quietly, and hoping for a sense of naturalness in his photographs.

AT HOME IN THE WHITE HOUSE

Following the election of 1960 children returned to the White House after nearly 50 years. Not since the Theodore Roosevelt Administration had young children been a part of White House life. The public clamored for news of John and Caroline's likes and dislikes, and sought Jackie's advice on parenting. Despite intense public interest, access was strictly regulated, and the children's privacy was protected under Jackie's watchful eye.

ABOVE: *August 1962. John Kennedy, Jr., plays with his mother's string of pearls.*
RIGHT: *November 1961. John Jr. and Caroline play in their new home, the White House.*

LETITIA BALDRIGE: The Kennedy children in the White House were just the tonic America needed after decades of older presidential families occupying the house. The public ate up every bit of information they could get on the children, including what they were eating, saying, and wearing. Even their haircuts became matters of national interest. Jackie tried her best to keep them away from the photographers' lenses, but when the First Lady was out riding in Virginia, the President would on rare occasions let the cameras into the room where he was playing with them. These photo ops were always at press secretary Pierre Salinger's instigation, knowing there would be great press the next day. It was a "cat and mouse" operation, with the press playing the role of the cat whenever they had a chance to get at the children, and with Jackie reacting with fury the next day.

LEFT: *April 1, 1963. John Jr. and Caroline attend a tea party on the White House lawn.*
ABOVE: *June 22, 1962. Caroline, John, and pony Macaroni pay a visit to the Oval Office.*

LETITIA BALDRIGE: The children were very much a part of their parents' lives. Every morning they would come down and see the President in his office before their day started. Every evening he would come and spend part of their suppertime with them. Jackie was with them all the time. She had so much privacy up in the family quarters—no one was ever allowed up there. She was really able to be with them, to see them grow. If she had been living in a house and had a job, she would have seen them much less than she saw them as First Lady. She raised them beautifully. Every time they went through the White House the Secret Service would clear the way and they would rush through. But of course tourists would get an occasional glimpse of 12 little girls in pink tutus, ballet skirts, and pink tights going out to dance on the South Lawn. Everybody was enchanted—they couldn't get enough of the children. And the Kennedys were smart, they kept them away from the press. And that made them even greater assets.

ABOVE: *May 7, 1963. Jackie lends a hand with Caroline's class at the White House school.*
RIGHT: *November 27, 1962. Caroline attends her birthday party in the Diplomatic Reception Room.*

HUGH SIDEY: Kids in the Kennedy White House softened the grave aura of international tension and spoke of the future and the perpetual youth and energy that Kennedy embodied. The pony Macaroni showed up on the White House porch. There were parties and picnics on the lawn. A tiny sleigh with kids aboard on a snow-dusted South Lawn was one year's Christmas card. Summer visits to Hyannis Port were as much a kids' camp as anything, with squealing rallies for ice cream and splashing in the weak surf. Kindergarten was on the third floor of the White House; Halloween goblins invaded the Oval Office. John Jr. found the trapdoor in the President's desk, opened it, and just by chance stared into a camera lens.

Caroline and John Jr. and their multitude of cousins and tiny friends, while protected from the prying camera lenses by Jackie, nevertheless paraded into public sightings at opportune times, often arranged and choreographed by the President. Caroline used to come over to the Oval Office and there was never any restraint. It didn't matter who was there; if she decided to go in, she did. You knew she would be dragging her doll along and Kennedy would be discussing the fate of the Western world … but he wouldn't tell her to go away. He would introduce the guests and she would just kind of hang around. Swipe a little candy from Mrs. Lincoln's desk. And then wander off. Kids on deck were a part of what would become the "Camelot Myth."

BARBARA BAKER BURROWS: Cecil Stoughton was the official White House photographer before the title even existed. Like his civilian counterparts who got most of the attention, Cecil captured the family as well as the President. "Pictures of the kids were most likely to be taken when Jackie was out of town." On an October day in 1962 the sounds of clapping and wailing from the Oval Office caught Cecil's attention. Beckoned in by the President as he sang and clapped, and the children danced, Cecil shot just 12 frames before heading to the lab.

"What have you got there, Captain?" quizzed Kennedy when Cecil returned that afternoon with a set of prints. Then, with the photographs on his desk and a huge smile on his face, the President pressed a button on the intercom. "Piaah," he summoned his press secretary in an exaggerated Boston-French, "Why can't we give these to the press?" [p. 183].

The pictures were splashed across front pages around the world. After unquestionably his most historic photograph [p. 195] Cecil considers these as important as any he has ever taken.

Look magazine's Stanley Tretick was another in the core group of photographers around the Kennedys. His photographs of John-John playing under his father's desk [following pages] are among the most memorable to show that special mix of the children and presidential life. With his great sense of humor, Stan used to tell of showing the President a rather large tray of photographs. Kennedy sat in his rocking chair, showing keen interest. With each slide would come a compliment: "That's wonderful, Stan." "Marvelous." And so it went through most of the tray—until: "You know, Stan, I'm not really fond of that one." As Stan put it, "He was so charming that he charmed the slide right out of the tray!"

LEFT: *November 27, 1960. Spectators strain for a glimpse of Caroline; her official doll carrier lags behind.*
FOLLOWING PAGES: *October 4, 1963. John Jr. plays on the floor of the Oval Office as his father talks to advisers and aides.*

AN ORDINARY FAMILY

Away from the White House, the dignitaries, and the hype, the Kennedy children were free to be normal children. John Jr. and Caroline spent much of their summers in Cape Cod playing with their many cousins and awaiting the weekend arrival of their father. In August 1963, the family shared a tragedy: the death of brother Patrick just days after his birth. The President flew all of the family dogs to Cape Cod for solace and comfort.

LEFT: *John and Caroline Kennedy aboard the Honey Fitz, summer 1963.*
ABOVE: *August 14, 1963. The first family and many of their dogs on the patio of their rented Squaw Island house near Hyannis Port.*

LETITIA BALDRIGE: The public wanted to be present for all John Kennedy family moments. They wanted a peek at their picnics, their sailing, swimming, trampoline-jumping, anything that could be shown to them. To the outside world, the spectacle of this attractive family at play with their dogs all over the place was downright celestial. They may have looked like staged photographs, and perhaps they were sometimes, but it did not matter. They were, after all, pictures of the Kennedys! Jackie remarked several times that she saw more of her husband after he was elected than she did during the campaign days. He was "home" in the White House, so they had more time together than during all the previous years when he always had to be somewhere else.

BARBARA BAKER BURROWS: Not previously in the 20th century had the White House been home to such small children (when the Kennedys moved in, Caroline was barely three, John-John a mere two months—his third birthday was to be the day of his father's funeral). And Jackie's pregnancy in 1963—although it ended sadly in the premature birth and only 39-hour life of son Patrick—reminded the country of just how young the inhabitants of the White House really were. Yet the children also served a vital role for the President. Remarking that "sometimes they even have lunch with him," Jackie observed: "After all, the one thing that happens to a President is that his ties with the outside world are cut, and the people you really have are each other."

LETITIA BALDRIGE: There is no normalcy when you try to raise children in the White House. There were always hordes of people around—clucking, questioning, staring at John and Caroline as though they were pandas in the zoo. This is exactly why Jackie kept the children away from the prying eyes of the press and the public.

What fascinated us was the amount of mail the children received—letters sent by other children, adults, celebrities, and people in prison. Here were numerous letters addressed to the children's animals, everyone from their dogs to their hamsters and from their ponies to the songbirds in their cages. I tried to have the letters answered as nicely as possible, signing my own name to them, not Mrs. Kennedy's. Otherwise, there would be no limit to the amount of animal fan mail, and we had enough human mail to handle as it was.

ROBERT DALLEK: The public has a boundless interest in presidential families. It is similar to its fascination with Hollywood actors or other celebrities. The public loves gossip about a President's relations with his wife and children and consumes every bit of information available about their daily lives. President Kennedy understood that his family was a political asset, especially his highly attractive children. He also understood that the public would be as interested in negative stories or scandals. Though, as is now well known, he was a womanizer, who had numerous affairs, he was careful to hide this from the public. Perhaps more to the point, he took advantage of the fact that in the 1960s, the media did not invade a President's private life the way it does now, or tries to. As a consequence, the public picture of him and his wife and children during his Presidency was of a model family that Americans could admire and even idealize.

RIGHT: *October 10, 1963. John Jr. follows his dad to work.*

CHAPTER 4

Glamorous Washington

n an interview with a high school newspaper reporter while still a senator, John F. Kennedy was asked if he had an "in" with *Life* magazine. "No," he replied, "I just have a beautiful wife." And although he may not have been telling the whole truth about his relationship with the magazine, he summed up an important part of his appeal. Jackie was unconventionally pretty, and her taste in clothes, artists, and people became trendsetting. She brought glamour and culture to the White House, and the guest list to match. She filled White House receptions, intimate and grand, with a "who's who" of names from the world of music and the arts. And when Jack Kennedy's Hollywood connections were added to the mix, Washington, D.C., came alive.

The Kennedys constantly graced the covers of magazines from *Time, Life, Look,* and *Parade,* to *U.S. News and World Report,* and the *Catholic Digest*—and it was no accident. They were attractive and surrounded themselves with other glamorous people—*newsworthy* glamorous people. With lunch guests like Princess Grace, it is no wonder photographs of the President and Mrs. Kennedy, like those of movie stars, beamed out from covers of magazines. The news organizations that featured the new American "royalty" knew that a Kennedy cover sold magazines and myths alike.

The first couple had always had big-name friends, acquaintances, and even relatives. Between the two of them, they counted a princess and actor Peter Lawford, of Hollywood's infamous Rat Pack, as members of the family. Jackie's sister, Lee (born Caroline Lee Bouvier), had married Polish Prince Stanislaw Radziwill in 1959, becoming a princess; and Jack's sister Pat had married Lawford, an MGM contract player, in 1954. Lawford, who helped link the Kennedy men to Hollywood, introduced the President to Marilyn Monroe.

Jack's Hollywood connections were on display throughout the 1960 presidential race. The list of celebrities who participated in radio and television commercials for Kennedy is dazzling: Harry Belafonte, Lena Horne, Milton Berle, Gene Kelly, Henry Fonda, Myrna Loy, and many others. So it was fitting that in 1960 the Democratic National Convention should take place in Los Angeles, the city where Democratic fund-raising events had already been drawing guests like Marlon Brando, Burt Lancaster, Dean Martin, Jack Webb, and Cary Grant. At the opening of the convention, the delegates were treated to a star-studded rendition of the "Star-Spangled Banner," performed by Peter Lawford, Sammy Davis, Jr., Shirley MacLaine, and, of course, Ol' Blue Eyes himself.

At John F. Kennedy's Inauguration, the cultural heights his administration would seek became clear. Kennedy invited artists Marian Anderson and Robert Frost to perform. That Marian Anderson would sing the "Star-Spangled Banner" to commemorate the dawn of the New Frontier was not lost on black Americans. After the complacency of the Eisenhower years, this symbolic embrace of the struggle for equality was meaningful for many Americans. Kennedy did not immediately follow up his gesture with major support for the civil rights movement, but as with his other PR efforts, the acknowledgement became part of his mystique and he remained a beloved figure in much of the black community.

Much to the chagrin of PR-hungry politicians scrambling for the best seats at the Inauguration, they had to compete with 50 or so representatives of the artistic elite. W. H. Auden, Robert Lowell, John Hersey, Alexis Léger, Allen Tate, and John Steinbeck were all among the guests Kennedy invited. It was the first time that the Kennedys hosted such a high caliber group of writers, artists, and performers, but by no means the last.

LEFT: *January 20, 1961. The President and First Lady leave the White House to attend the Inaugural Balls.*
PREVIOUS PAGES: *August 6, 1962. The National Capitol Symphony Orchestra and Ballet performs on the South Lawn.*

Over the course of the Kennedy Administration, Jackie would be idolized as a sort of self-appointed cultural czarina. As the *New York Times* put it, she was "well-qualified for the role of unofficial Minister of Culture." Throughout the 1960 presidential primary, and a full year into the Kennedys' tenure in the White House, Jackie was targeted for severe criticism because of European tastes and devotion to haute couture. Critics slammed her pricey wardrobe during the campaign, with publications like *Women's Wear Daily* suggesting that she was running on the "Paris couture fashion ticket."

To damp down the criticism, Jack imposed an American-only clothing policy on his wife. Jackie responded by appointing Oleg Cassini her personal designer. It was a clever call. Russian by descent, but raised in Italy, Cassini had spent more than 20 years in America designing for—and romancing—Hollywood actresses Gene Tierney and Grace Kelly. He created a name for himself in Hollywood and on Broadway, and was the perfect choice for Jackie: American enough to satisfy her critics and European enough to satisfy her tastes.

THE PRESIDENT AND FIRST LADY PREPARE TO WELCOME THE PRESIDENT OF MOROCCO.

As First Lady, Jacqueline Kennedy used her particular talents to raise the cultural bar of the White House and, by extension, the entire country; her interest in European literature and history, her abiding interest in the arts, her facility with foreign languages, and, especially, her love for French fashion and food became hallmarks of her unique style. In time, these became the very characteristics for which she was adored.

Jackie was dismayed by the state of the White House. After the election and the birth of her son John, a frail Jackie accepted Mamie Eisenhower's offer of a tour of the White House. Too intimidated to request the wheelchair that they had ready and waiting for her, Jackie suffered through the tour on foot. Upset by the mediocre reproductions of period furniture and the lack of iconic pieces highlighting the house's historic significance, Jackie flew to Palm Beach, Florida, to recover from the difficult birth, and plot her strategy. She simply refused to be surrounded by cheap, shoddy furniture, cold, gloomy rooms, and impersonal entertaining spaces, and vowed to transform the White House into an emblematic building worthy of the country's pride.

While in Palm Beach, she had the Library of Congress send book after book about the history of the White House. She wasn't starting from scratch. Before she moved in as First Lady, Jackie had been keeping lists, writing memos, and seeking answers to questions about the White House. She was particular about her aims. "It would be a sacrilege merely to 'redecorate'—a word I hate," she told Hugh Sidey in an interview for *Life*. "It must be restored and that has nothing to do with decoration." She created the White House Historical Association, appointed a curator, and solicited influential people for a Committee of the Fine Arts Commission for the White House. Jackie also supported legislation extending the White House museum status, thus enabling it to receive gifts and donations.

To showcase the renovation, Jackie worked hard on the creation of a White House guidebook. *The White House: An Historic Guide*, still in print today, was the first official handbook of the White House. The book was a big hit. What followed would amount to a smashing success.

In addition to the publication of the guide, Jackie staged a televised tour of the White House, one of the most successful public relations events ever undertaken by the Kennedys. In January 1962, a crew of 40 from CBS television, tons of equipment in tow, descended on Washington, D.C. Mrs. Kennedy rehearsed for a day, then spent two days filming. She did not work from a script. Instead, the First Lady led viewers on a stroll through the White House, answering correspondent Charles Collingswood's questions on-the-fly, and speaking extemporaneously about each room and its wonderful furnishings and decorations.

Mindful of critics, and her reputation as a big spender, she quelled fears that she might have embarked on the ambitious White House makeover simply to satisfy her own highbrow tastes. She assured the public that she wanted the White House to be a place of pilgrimage for all Americans. But as much as Jackie wanted Americans to know that the Kennedys were immensely proud of their American heritage, she wanted the world to know it, too, so she recorded the show in French and Spanish so that it could be broadcast abroad. Entitled "A Tour of the White House with Mrs. John F. Kennedy," the one-hour program aired on CBS on Valentine's Day 1962, then again on ABC and NBC four days later. Fifty-six million Americans tuned in.

After sharing her home with millions of Americans, Jackie's popularity skyrocketed. The guidebook and the renewed interest in the state of the White House were clearly factors in the rise of tourists visiting the presidential site. In 1962, nearly two-thirds more people visited the White House than in 1960. Both through their entertaining of world leaders and in this televised tour of their home, the Kennedys were helping to change the perception of America abroad.

Back when she had been recuperating in Palm Beach, Jackie did more than brainstorm the changes in White House décor. She also made notes about how she wanted to entertain in her new home. She wanted to put her best foot forward, which meant emphasizing the things she knew well. "The entertaining is going to be very important to us," she said to Letitia Baldrige. It was something of an understatement.

In her time as a Senate wife, Jackie was already an accomplished hostess and political wife, and she began to put these talents to use in the White House. She replaced long, impersonal tables with cozier round

tables. Seating eight or ten guests at a time, the tables allowed for easy conversation among those present. She kept the music low or absent, often split up husbands and wives, and carefully planned seating arrangements to encourage discussions among guests. Probably the most notable change she made in the area of entertaining was her appointment of Frenchman René Verdon as the White House chef.

The Kennedys' private luncheons, intimate dinners, and enormous state functions, as well as the elegant entertainment they chose and stunning guest lists they assembled, dazzled the American public. Never before had a presidential couple so awed the world, as much with their entertaining as with their political message. She thoroughly planned each event, laying out intricate seating charts, vetting menus against what she knew of guests' food preferences and needs. America was soon won over by her exquisite and informed tastes. People copied her in every way they could. "Mrs. Kennedy had such marvelous taste ... that all the women across the country copied her ... that little pillbox ... the sleeveless shift. It was an epidemic, that wardrobe," Betty Ford once remarked.

Look magazine summed up "Jackie's revolution" in a January 1962 article: "Washington is striving to erase a long-held notion—that, compared to other world capitals, it's a cultural hick town where there's nothing to do at night. The White House has set a new tone in making it an agreeable and fashionable civic duty to encourage the arts."

The Kennedys hosted numerous evenings dedicated to showcasing the arts. Renowned cellist Pablo Casals's performance at the White House was among the most

THE NEW PRESIDENT, THE YOUNGEST IN AMERICAN HISTORY, WAS INSTANTLY A SUBJECT OF GREAT INTEREST TO THE MEDIA. HE APPEARS HERE ON A SPECIAL EDITION OF *TIME*.

notable. But there were many others. Leonard Bernstein and Vladimir Nabokov topped the guest list at a dinner for Igor Stravinsky; and the Jerome Robbins ballet company performed for the Shah and Empress of Iran. Composer Leonard Bernstein was impressed with the "feeling of hospitality, of warmth, of welcome, the taste with which everything was done, the goodness of everything ... the food is marvelous, the wines are delicious, there are cigarettes on the table, people are laughing, laughing out loud, telling stories, jokes, enjoying themselves, glad to be there."

Under Jackie's keen eye, entertainment at the White House flourished. She hosted poetry readings, Shakespeare plays, operas, ballets, and jazz performances. The Kennedys were the first couple to encourage young people to study, play, and appreciate music. They also held the first dinner for all remaining recipients of the congressional Medal of Honor, and a special evening for Nobel laureates, an affair that boasted 49 Nobel Prize winners and a laundry list of jaw-dropping names and faces. From Linus Pauling and Robert Oppenheimer to Pearl Buck and Robert Frost, the night brought together some of the greatest minds in the world. Authors James Baldwin, John Dos Passos, and Katherine Anne Porter, astronaut John Glenn, and Ernest Hemingway's widow, Mary, also attended the reception.

After dinner that evening, legendary actor Frederic March entertained the heady crowd in the East Room. He read the introduction to Sinclair Lewis's *Main Street*, and passages from former Secretary of State George Marshall's address to Harvard University in which he laid out the Marshall Plan. Finally, in the presence of Marshall's and Hemingway's widows, March intoned a chapter from an unpublished work by Ernest Hemingway. In his description of the unforgettable evening, *Vanity Fair* reporter William Styron wrote, "Jack and Jackie actually shimmered. You would have to be abnormal, perhaps psychotic, to be immune to their dumbfounding appeal. Even Republicans were gaga. They were truly the golden couple, and I am not trying to play down my own sense of wonder when I note that a number of the guests, male and female, appeared so affected by the glamour that their eyes took on a goofy, catatonic glaze."

One of the most esteemed guests of the Kennedy White House was French writer and statesman André Malraux. Before being appointed minister of information, then minister of state for cultural affairs by French President de Gaulle, Malraux lived a very colorful life, getting arrested in Cambodia for removing art from a Khmer Temple, editing an anti-colonialist newspaper in Saigon, fighting in the Spanish Civil War, and actively serving in the Resistance during World War II. When the Kennedys visited Paris in 1961, Malraux spent time with Jackie, accompanying her to the Jeu de Paume and Malmaison despite having lost his two sons in a car accident just days before. They developed a friendship that grew each time they saw one another.

Of the more than 160 guests invited to share the evening with Malraux were distinguished playwrights Arthur Miller, Tennessee Williams, Thornton Wilder, and Paddy Chayefsky, as well as Pulitzer Prize–winning poets and writers Archibald MacLeish, Robert Lowell, and Robert Penn Warren. Other bright lights of the art world who came to the White House for the special reception in May 1962 were Leonard Bernstein, dancer and choreographer Agnes de Mille, painters Andrew Wyeth and Mark Rothko, director Elia Kazan, writer Saul Bellow, actress Julie Harris, acting teacher Lee Strasberg, and

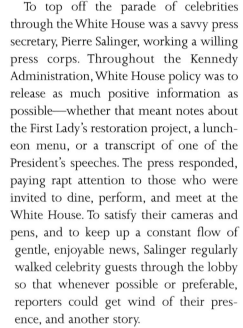

JACKIE'S WHITE HOUSE RESTORATION PLANS WERE FEATURED IN THE SEPTEMBER 1, 1961, ISSUE OF *LIFE*.

choreographer extraordinaire George Balanchine. At the end of this glittering evening, a giddy Jacqueline Kennedy remarked, "These are the moments of history I will really remember the rest of my life." André Malraux must also have been charmed; shortly after his visit to the White House, he agreed to allow one of France's greatest masterpieces, Leonardo da Vinci's "Mona Lisa," to travel from the Louvre to Washington for a much hyped exhibit.

To top off the parade of celebrities through the White House was a savvy press secretary, Pierre Salinger, working a willing press corps. Throughout the Kennedy Administration, White House policy was to release as much positive information as possible—whether that meant notes about the First Lady's restoration project, a luncheon menu, or a transcript of one of the President's speeches. The press responded, paying rapt attention to those who were invited to dine, perform, and meet at the White House. To satisfy their cameras and pens, and to keep up a constant flow of gentle, enjoyable news, Salinger regularly walked celebrity guests through the lobby so that whenever possible or preferable, reporters could get wind of their presence, and another story.

In the Kennedy White House, Princess Grace or Kirk Douglas might just as easily be a guest for dinner as the prime minister of Canada; the President might be lounging poolside with Bing Crosby as easily as he might be discussing civil rights policy with Bobby. Time and again, high-profile and glamorous personalities stood alongside the Kennedys, and their wining and dining of the political, artistic, and Hollywood elite had a palpable and lasting effect on the way Americans viewed the first family, the Presidency, and themselves.

GLAMOUR COMES TO WASHINGTON

On January 20, 1961, Washington welcomed the Kennedys with no fewer than five Inaugural Balls, despite the wintry weather. Dressed in white tie and tails, the new President cut a dashing figure through the flurry of parties. But it was Jackie whose carefully chosen yet deceptively simple white gown stole the show. Clearly a new age of glamour had come to the Capitol.

HUGH SIDEY: Good looks and money are important ingredients of glamour, but the glamour that the Kennedys created went far beyond that. The Kennedy Presidency furnished the global power and intrigue that often enhance glamour. The allure that Jackie rounded out was made up of the best in art, music, theater, literature, and food. There was another side, too, which deepened fascination. Private parties with close friends and no reporters often went into the wee hours. The outside world never caught a glimpse of the conga lines and the twist, but word was whispered and many would have swooned for an invitation. Few made it.

LETITIA BALDRIGE: The Inaugural gala concert organized by Frank Sinatra and the Hollywoodians he brought along was the kickoff to a frenetic schedule of events for the Kennedys. There were great discussions over which dress she would wear which night because there were two rather sensational new ones hanging in her closet. She chose the one pictured above, a heavy satin French designer dress to wear to the gala. She stepped out of their Georgetown house into a blinding snowstorm, a vision in white, and found a huge crowd waiting for her in the terrible cold. She did not disappoint her fans. They looked stunned when she appeared.

LEFT: January 19, 1961. Jacqueline Kennedy steps into the snow for a night of pre-Inaugural celebrations.
ABOVE: January 20, 1961. The presidential box overlooked thousands of dancing celebrants at the National Guard Armory.
FOLLOWING PAGES: January 19, 1961. Frank Sinatra leads stars in song, including Nat King Cole, Harry Belafonte, Ella Fitzgerald, and Gene Kelly.

TRANSFORMING THE WHITE HOUSE

Disappointed that few items in the White House reflected America's rich history, Jackie set to work on the ambitious task of restoring 1600 Pennsylvania Avenue. Before the Inauguration she formed a restoration committee and invited Henry du Pont, who had created the Winterthur museum in Delaware, to chair the effort. With the help of a team of curators, Jackie located numerous priceless items, including a set of Abraham Lincoln's china, a table purchased by James Monroe for the Blue Room, and two rugs specially ordered by Theodore Roosevelt. In February 1962, the First Lady hosted a televised tour of the restored White House. Room by room, she reintroduced America to its presidential past. In June of that year the White House Historical Association published a guide to the White House that sold more than 600,000 copies. *House and Garden* magazine praised the First Lady's effort, calling the restoration "Washington's most inspiring example of the juxtaposition of charm and grandeur."

ABOVE: *Jackie assists in the positioning of a Monroe-era candelabrum in the Blue Room.*
RIGHT: *January 15, 1962. Jackie discusses the White House renovations for her CBS special.*

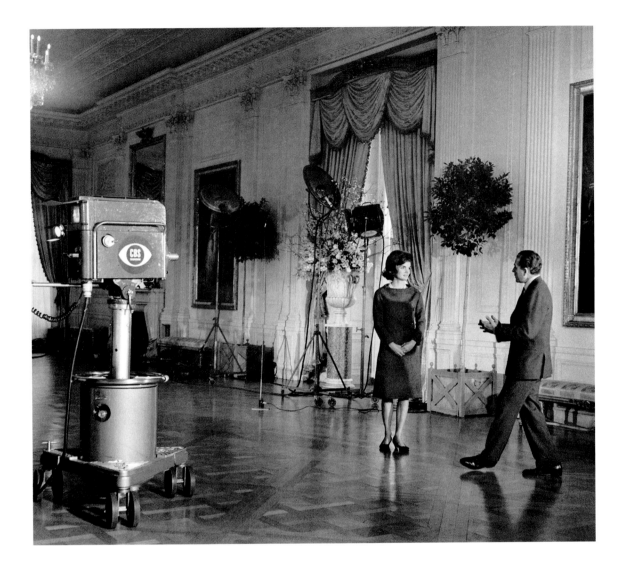

LETITIA BALDRIGE: Jackie was so well prepared for the CBS tour of the White House. She ripped through all the historic rooms in her little red suit—the Red Room, the Green Room, the Blue Room—she knew the story behind every portrait, every piece of furniture. It woke America up to the fact that we had a great piece of history right there at 1600 Pennsylvania Avenue. We didn't have a castle, but our heads of state lived in a very historic, very American house. And after the television special, everyone had to see it. There must have been 100,000 people a month who tried to get in to see the rooms.

ABOVE: The President's rocking chair sits in an Oval Office that reflects his nautical interests.

ABOVE: The restored Blue Room, the main reception room of the White House during the Kennedy Administration.

A NEW WAY TO ENTERTAIN

Thanks to a number of innovations, an invitation to the White House soon became one of the most sought-after requests in town. The First Lady introduced more intimate seating arrangements, flattering lighting, French cuisine, and a glittering guest list to White House parties. Photographs of the events—and Jackie's elegant dresses—were published all over the world. The Kennedys welcomed hundreds of foreign dignitaries as well as a host of writers, artists, and other art world luminaries to the White House. All would carry away memories of magical evenings.

LETITIA BALDRIGE: When the Kennedys chose to give the state dinner for Gen. Ayub Khan, President of Pakistan, at George Washington's estate in Virginia, a new precedent was set, both for the White House and for Mount Vernon. The Vice-Regents, a formidable group of ladies from different states who are active trustees and protectors of the estate, had never allowed any group to use the house. It was sacrosanct ground, but for the Kennedys they relented. Although this wasn't Versailles, it was just as historic and memorable to the Americans for an important state dinner. The food was prepared in the White House and trucked out to Mount Vernon, complete with refrigeration and heating equipment. The guests were transported from Washington up the Potomac on PT boats, a reminder of John F. Kennedy's war service. There was a welcoming ceremony on the piazza in front of the house where troops, dressed in Revolutionary Army uniforms, performed a military drill that Washington himself had designed. Guests drank mint juleps made according to Washington's own recipe, in highly polished pewter cups, just as they used in the late 1770s. Dinner was served in a beautiful tent overlooking the river. The National Symphony Orchestra performed a concert after dinner in a natural theater on the grounds. It was history repeating history, and the Kennedys made their own history by producing this state dinner. Pakistan was a new and important ally of the United States, and President Ayub Khan was immensely honored by this unique celebration.

LEFT: *July 11, 1961. The President and Mrs. Kennedy host a state dinner for President Ayub Khan of Pakistan at Mount Vernon.*
ABOVE: *Natural flowers, Porthault linens, and beautiful place settings were among many entertaining innovations during the Kennedy years.*

LETITIA BALDRIGE: The extremely attractive young couple in the White House had suddenly made all of the crowned heads of Europe look drab in comparison. The Kennedys received official invitations to visit almost every country in the world, and those countries in return lobbied the State Department constantly for an invitation from the White House. There weren't enough days in the year to accommodate them all. The state visit competition was fierce!

BARBARA BAKER BURROWS: In contrast to what the *New York Times* described as "the almost cloistered existence led by Presidents of the past," photographs revealed the new Kennedy Administration to be active and involved. "That dreary *maison blanche*," Jackie called the White House. First Ladies might be expected to redecorate, but Jackie, the student of art and history, wanted to give the nation a presidential home in keeping with its stature. And within that White House came state dinners and concerts, a whole world of culture that spilled out over Washington and beyond.

BELOW: *April 11, 1962. Jackie dazzles in a simple gown as the Kennedys welcome the Shah and Empress of Iran to the White House.*
RIGHT: *May 11, 1962. Jackie's gown is the center of attention at a ceremony to welcome French Minister of Culture André Malraux.*

EMBRACING CULTURE

Jacqueline Kennedy's passion for the finer things in life inspired an influx of culture to the White House. After-dinner entertainment ranged from classical piano to modern dance to Shakespeare readings. Members of the art community became valued White House guests. The Kennedys entertained French Minister of Culture André Malraux, who helped arrange for the "Mona Lisa" exhibit at the National Gallery in 1963. On one memorable evening in April 1962, 49 Nobel laureates and other luminaries, including Pearl Buck and Robert Frost, were honored in a special reception.

ABOVE: *January 8, 1963. Jackie Kennedy and André Malraux attend the opening of the "Mona Lisa" exhibition at the National Gallery.*
RIGHT: *April 11, 1962. Jerome Robbins's ballet performs for the Shah and Empress of Iran in the East Room.*
FOLLOWING PAGES: *Physicist Linus Pauling waltzes at the White House.*

LETITIA BALDRIGE: Jackie used to take Caroline to the dress rehearsal of any scheduled ballets, and the little girl was very disappointed to hear that these "workout sweats," not costumes, were to be worn for the actual performance. Modern dance was striving for realism by now, and fancy costumes were on their way out!

ROBERT DALLEK: Kennedy embraced the arts during his Presidency, partly in response to Jacqueline's affinity for high culture. While he genuinely shared his wife's regard for the life of the mind, Kennedy also understood that it was smart politics. White House promotion of the arts encouraged Americans to feel superior to a Khrushchev-led Soviet Union, where free expression and refined taste were in short supply.

ABOVE: *June 1, 1961. Jackie wears an elegant navy silk suit for lunch with Chief Mayor Julien Tardieu at the Hotel de Ville, Paris.*
RIGHT: *Enraptured by the First Lady, Indians dubbed Jackie "Ameriki Rani, Queen of America."*

LETITIA BALDRIGE: Jackie's great sense of style was based on appropriateness. She always chose the right thing to wear for any occasion. In France, with the President on her way to lunch with the mayor, she wore a navy silk suit and hat, very businesslike, and with her hat and ever present white gloves, she was properly dressed for lunch at the Hotel de Ville.

In India, of course, the entire world waited for the photo of Jackie in front of the exquisite Taj Mahal. It was very hot, but she looked cool as a cucumber in her sleeveless sheath printed with Indian art figures. And of course the short white gloves and stunning black and amber necklace. *Just right.*

STAR POWER

It didn't take long for Kennedy mania to sweep the nation. While Eisenhower supporters had worn "I like Ike" badges for the previous President, enthusiasm for JFK and his wife reached stratospheric proportions; Jack and Jackie Kennedy had become celebrity politicians. Kennedy Halloween masks, life-size mannequins, and a spot-on JFK impersonator were among the more well-known manifestations of Kennedy mania. Few can deny the extraordinary effect of Jackie's style of hair and dress, which had a profound impact on fashion in the era. Women rushed to adopt Jackie's simple and elegant style of dress and flattering hairstyle, inspiring *Ladies Home Journal* to write: "Jackie's slightest fashion whim triggers seismic tremors up and down Seventh Avenue."

RIGHT: January 20, 1961. Mannequins of the Kennedys designed for a New York department store draw stares on the street.
ABOVE September 6, 1962. The President and First Lady depart a performance of Irving Berlin's musical Mr. President at Washington's National Theater. Alice Roosevelt Longworth, daughter of Theodore Roosevelt, is visible behind the Kennedys.

BARBARA BAKER BURROWS: The social era of the "60s" was not definitively set by the calendar, but it certainly received a cultural and stylistic nudge from the Kennedys. It only took the listing of *From Russia With Love* among his reading preferences for the President to help make a sensation of a little-known British spy. Women fitted themselves out in Jackie fashions. Even Bob Dylan sang about the power of the "Leopard-Skin Pill-Box Hat." The Kennedy style was contagious.

ROBERT DALLEK: The President and Jacqueline became America's most famous celebrities in the sixties. It was not just their standing as chief executive and First Lady that made them popular with Americans but their huge, glamorous family, which gathered with its many children to celebrate birthdays, play touch football, and live the good life. The Kennedys had become America's royal family, and Kennedy mimicry became a national pastime during his Presidency.

BARBARA BAKER BURROWS: As early as 1937, Life magazine ran a full two-page portrait of Joe Kennedy's very large and handsome family. The headline read: "Nine Children and Nine Million Dollars." Despite the family's share of tragedy, the press coverage that followed pictured an American success. For JFK, his looks, wit, and charm were givens, but without the accompanying wealth there might have been no Harvard education, no wandering Europe, the ambassador's son researching his first book, and little financing for those early campaigns. But the family prospered, and Jacqueline Bouvier added something more. Surrounded by the trappings of wealth, the continuously photographed family was the very image of an attractive and affluent lifestyle. Together, their natural and earned assets made for an unbeatable combination, the raw ingredients of the Kennedy mystique.

ROBERT DALLEK: Although Kennedy wealth was an important part of the national admiration for Jack, Jackie, and the whole family, the mystique rested on more than that. It also grew out of the feeling that the Kennedys set a high standard for themselves and the country—that excellence in everything they did should stand as the model for all Americans in work and leisure.

LEFT: November 1963. The President and First Lady relax at the Kennedy family retreat in Atoka, Virginia.
ABOVE: The Kennedys watch the 21st America's Cup race, Newport, Rhode Island.

LEFT: *May 19, 1962. Marilyn Monroe sings "Happy Birthday" to the President in a televised special.*
ABOVE: *May 24, 1961. Princess Grace of Monaco casts an admiring glance at the President.*

HUGH SIDEY: John Kennedy was not Hollywood handsome, explained a friend, "just damned manly and good looking." But there was something more. There was a kindness in his eyes and manner. Perhaps it came from his experience in the war or maybe from years of illness as a young man; an understanding that other people might have bad luck by the accident of birth, or that as he so honestly put it, "life is unfair." Men responded when he stood on the back of a car and shouted his message to try to ease that unfairness. For older women he was the son they wanted, for younger women—well, he was beyond calculation. When watching from behind Kennedy, one could see that each person in the crowd in front felt Kennedy was talking to them. When he dove into those seas of admirers, anyone lucky enough to meet him face to face saw warmth and a crinkled smile and felt a firm handshake like that of a friend. And always for these largely female clusters there was an overlay of magnetism, the hint of some wild adventure if he would only meet them in their dreams.

BARBARA BAKER BURROWS: There were two Jackies. We saw one die, a glamorous woman who had sought privacy but became one of the most photographed people in the world. We saw her raise her children, do meaningful work, and begin to age gracefully. It's likely though, that it will be the other, an earlier Jackie, who passes into the future.

In *Life*'s 25th-anniversary issue, published in 1961, among chapters on major events and movies and war, there is one titled "An Abundance of Beauty." Page follows page of pinups and stars and, on the very last—Jackie. Her inclusion, startling then, is a powerful reminder so many administrations later: She had already transcended to become a star. It was a celebrity that only grew in the two years that followed. Then, when it all stopped, she helped hold a nation together. And, as we tried to understand, it was her comparison to Camelot of the life that had just ended for her husband, for their country, that would concentrate the Kennedy mystique. It was also to be her eulogy. Like any life prematurely ended, the record of what was and, particularly, the promise of what might come is everything we have left.

LETITIA BALDRIGE: I remember that Jacqueline Kennedy, beginning in her teens, was always reserved in public, far less so in private. As the wife of the President, she understood and accepted her duty to the press and to the nation to allow full coverage of her official activities, but she also held fast to the decree that the press was not to interject themselves into her private family life. This enticed the public even more. She became a woman of mystery, Greta Garbo-like. The more she said "no" to interviews and photo ops, the more the public wanted to see her and read about her.

One of the reporters teased her once for not being more cooperative with the press, when once she had been an "inquiring photographer" with a Washington newspaper after graduating from college. Another reporter standing nearby laughed and said, "Of course everyone cooperated with her and could hardly wait to be photographed and interviewed by her. Can you imagine anyone turning down an interview request from Jacqueline Bouvier?"

LEFT: *April 1961. Jacqueline Kennedy, photographed by Mark Shaw.*
PREVIOUS PAGES: *October 19, 1963. President Kennedy smokes a cigar at a Democratic fund-raising dinner at Boston University.*

CHAPTER 5

Broadcasting Success, Broadcasting Failure

As the White House went from black and white to Technicolor, so too did the country with images of the civil rights movement, Castro's Cuba, and the Soviet space race broadcast on every channel. America was getting its first practical view of the incredible power of television as well as photography. Now the public saw and heard far more than they ever had before. As much as the media helped the President, it also created intense pressure for an administration whose successes and failures were scrutinized daily. And early on, despite the steady string of PR and image-making successes that catapulted John F. Kennedy into the White House, the Kennedy Administration made its share of mistakes.

Shortly after the Bay of Pigs disaster in April 1961, President Kennedy stood before a crowd from the American Newspaper Publishers Association at the Waldorf-Astoria and asked "every publisher, every editor, and every newsman in the nation to reexamine his own standards, and to recognize the nature of our country's peril." He spoke of the press's wartime spirit of cooperation with the Chief Executive, and suggested "if the press is awaiting a declaration of war before it imposes self-discipline of combat conditions, then I can only say that no war ever posed a greater threat to our security." Looking for voluntary cooperation in the Cold War's gray areas, he told his audience, "Every newspaper now asks itself, with respect to every story: 'Is it news?' All I suggest is that you add the question: 'Is it in the interests of national security?'"

Many members of the press were incensed, believing his words were a clear rebuke for having run stories about Cuban exiles being trained in Florida prior to the Bay of Pigs debacle. For the remainder of Kennedy's turbulent tenure in office, his administration's successes and failures would be displayed on the cover of every magazine, in the headline of each newspaper, and in the leading story of the nightly news. In positive stories and stinging ones, the actions of the administration and the Kennedys would be under the watchful eyes of the media.

On August 13, 1961, East German security forces began installing barricades and barbed wire along the East Berlin border. The building of the Berlin Wall and the deepening trouble in the Eastern Bloc became a focal point in the war of images and intentions. Since World War II, Berlin had been a divided city. England, France, and the United States occupied West Berlin, and the Soviets controlled East Berlin. A steady stream of the most skilled workers fled East Germany every day, and Eastern Bloc inhabitants used Berlin as a comparatively easy corridor to the West. Angry at the loss of their most educated and productive people, the Soviets needed to halt the flow. In Vienna in 1961, Khrushchev declared that if a new arrangement was not worked out regarding Berlin by the end of the year, the Soviet Union would sign a separate peace agreement with East Berlin, marooning the city in a sea of Soviet influence. Ominously, Khrushchev declared, "If the U.S. wants to start a war over Germany, let it be so."

The threat of a nuclear exchange remained very real, and tensions took a turn for the worse in September when the Soviets renewed their nuclear testing program in Siberia. Kennedy was livid and, in turn, ordered the resumption of underground nuclear testing programs in the U.S. At the same time, he urged the Soviet Union and Britain to join him and agree to a ban on atmospheric nuclear tests. Correspondence between Washington and

LEFT: *Jacques Lowe portrait of John F. Kennedy.*
PREVIOUS PAGES: *January 19, 1961. President-elect John F. Kennedy talks to reporters on the day before the Inauguration.*

the Kremlin continued, and small steps were taken toward peaceful coexistence in Germany. It was Khrushchev who made the final step away from the brink, announcing that he would no longer insist on his end-of-the-year deadline. Kennedy remained distrustful of Khrushchev, but welcomed his retreat from hard-line threats. The Berlin crisis had been defused.

At the same time, Vietnam was becoming an increasingly visible hot spot. After the Vietnamese defeated the French colonialists in 1954, the country was divided pursuant to the Geneva Accords. Eisenhower pledged American support to the South Vietnamese government of Ngo Dinh Diem, hoping, of course, that the ruler would lean toward democratic reforms. When Kennedy took office, there were approximately 600 "advisers" in the small Southeast Asian nation. The situation was far from ideal—Ngo's absolutism and repression, as well as his appointment of his sadistic brother, Ngo Dinh Nhu, as his chief adviser did nothing to unify the South. In what was essentially a civil war between a communist North led by Ho Chi Minh and the "democratic" South, the United States became increasingly involved. By the end of 1963, some 800 "advisers" had grown to nearly 20,000 troops. Kennedy did not fancy sending in more. But with the belligerence of the Soviet Union and the situation in Berlin, he deemed it best to maintain the American obligation in Vietnam.

Kennedy's shining hour in the perilous realm of world events occurred during the Cuban missile crisis. The

U.S. AND SOVIET TANKS FACE OFF OVER THE NEWLY BUILT BERLIN WALL, AUGUST, 1961.

President had made it clear to Khrushchev that any Soviet buildup in Cuba would be viewed as a threat to the security of America and its allies, yet Khrushchev began clandestinely sending nuclear weapons to Cuba.

On October 14, 1962, a U-2 spy mission captured aerial photography of the installation of Soviet missile sites near San Cristóbal. Kennedy convened his most trusted advisers to develop a strategy for utilizing his strategic advantage (Khrushchev was unaware the photos existed) and rendering the weapons unusable—either by persuading the Soviets to remove them, or by a decisive Pearl Harbor-like attack.

Over the course of 13 days that would bring the world to the brink of nuclear devastation, Kennedy devised a plan that gave Khrushchev a way out. He ordered a naval "quarantine" to prevent the delivery of additional Soviet weapons. By leaving nonmilitary avenues open, but maintaining a firm stand, he held the moral high ground before an international audience.

As American warships patrolled the quarantine line, and Jack and Bobby struggled with the knowledge that millions of Americans might be wiped out in an impending nuclear war, the Soviets halted the ships headed for Cuba. Khrushchev backed down. He sent a message to the White House and, through a series of clandestine, often contradictory missives, the two leaders came to an agreement. It averted an American invasion of Cuba and, more important, nuclear holocaust.

Television's ever expanding news coverage of these and other events was a blessing and a curse. Just as the burgeoning medium of TV helped to elect Kennedy and project his image across America and the world, it amplified his troubles and those plaguing the country, particularly the escalating racial crisis. Televised images of Birmingham, Alabama, Police Commissioner Eugene "Bull" Connor's snarling police dogs and high-pressure fire hoses turned on nonviolent, civil rights demonstrators forced the public, and the President, to acknowledge the plight of black Americans in the South. The coverage of the clashes helped to produce a great change in the mood of the country. The escalating crisis, illustrated by a steady stream of negative images, would eventually force the President to act.

Kennedy's initial restraint did nothing to endear him to the civil rights leaders who helped to elect him. Martin Luther King, Jr., wrote a report on civil rights in *The Nation* in March 1962 subtitled "Fumbling on the New Frontier." Referring to Kennedy's campaign lambasting of Eisenhower, that Ike could have eliminated housing discrimination "with the stroke of his pen," civil rights groups began sending scores of pens to the White House.

The trouble was far from over. When King and groups from the Southern Christian Leadership Conference descended on Birmingham, Alabama, they were treated to more Southern racism and brutality at the hands of Bull Connor. In May, protesters marched against the city's continued illegal segregation. Police dogs were used to intimidate them. Fire hoses knocked protesters to the ground and tore their clothing. The President

IMAGES OF THE ONGOING STRUGGLE FOR CIVIL RIGHTS IN NEWSPAPERS AND ON TELEVISION BROUGHT THE CRISIS HOME.

acknowledged that an image on the news of a dog lunging at a teenager's midsection made him "sick." He was not the only one appalled by the violence that was being broadcast throughout the world. How could Kennedy combat Moscow's appeal in the developing world if this was how American citizens were treated in their own country?

While Kennedy sought a compromise with Connor, Martin Luther King penned his eloquent "Letter from Birmingham Jail" to white clergy. Many members of the civil rights movement were poised to abandon their commitment to nonviolence. Robert Kennedy warned of the violence that might soon erupt in cities across the nation if the situation was not brought under control. He eventually hammered out an agreement in Alabama, desegregating water fountains, department store dressing rooms, lunch counters, and restrooms, and guaranteeing some white-collar jobs to blacks. A committee was formed to monitor the situation and discuss further improvements.

Alabama's Governor George Wallace, known for his 1962 campaign mantra "segregation now, segregation tomorrow, segregation forever," swore he would rather rot in jail than permit integration at the University of Alabama, the only remaining segregated state university. Robert Kennedy was even roughed up when he went to Alabama to discuss the matter.

Finally, the President began preparing a civil rights bill for Congress. Worried about having adequate votes to pass the measure, the Kennedys came up with some effective PR initiatives to court public opinion, including inviting a documentary film crew to the White House. Both Kennedy men appeared calm, cool, and collected as they confidently discussed the growing crisis. George Wallace also permitted cameras to follow him before the big standoff at the University of Alabama, but he appeared nervous and jittery. Deputy Attorney General Nick Katzenbach was sent to Tuscaloosa to confront Wallace and enroll two students (Vivian Malone and James Hood) in the university. Knowing that every move would be captured on camera, Robert Kennedy instructed Katzenbach to "make him look ridiculous." Wallace, perched atop a wooden box for extra height, denied their entry, and Kennedy responded by federalizing the Alabama National Guard. Katzenbach returned in force, and the two black students were enrolled.

With victory in the ongoing civil rights struggle far from complete, Kennedy delivered a partly improvised speech that evening. On prime-time television, the Chief Executive addressed the moral issue of equality, which he said was "as old as the scriptures and as clear as the American Constitution." He tied his speech to his efforts abroad, saying, "This nation, for all its hopes and all its boasts will not be fully free until all its citizens are free." The day after he announced that he would be sending a civil rights bill to Congress, black activist Medgar Evers was shot and killed in front of his wife and children.

When the administration learned of the 1963 March on Washington being planned by A. Philip Randolph and Dr. King, the President opposed it flat out. What if it got out of control and jeopardized the rights bill? What if it

NIKITA KHRUSHCHEV—AND THE THREAT OF NUCLEAR WAR— APPEARED ON THE COVER OF *TIME* ON SEPTEMBER 8, 1961.

made him look the fool for his support of the movement? When it became clear that the march would go on with or without his support, he decided the only hope was to co-opt it as much as possible. Convinced that any missteps at the march would cause the failure of his civil rights bill (and of his Presidency), he put Bobby in charge of making it a harmonious rally rather than a protest gathering. Culminating in King's soaring "I Have a Dream" speech, the event could not have gone better.

It took Kennedy until 1963 to fulfill the promise he made during his campaign, and though it was a weaker law than movement leaders desired, it was a step in the right direction. The law, like the measures taken to protect civil rights demonstrators and the students integrating the South, would not have happened when it did had it not been for the press coverage and ensuing public outrage that shamed the government into taking a stand.

Just as photos of the lovely Kennedy family in the White House pleased the nation, images of the strong, energetic President tamed fears about the precarious state of world affairs. Sadly, the image of the spry, vigorous President couldn't be further from the truth. One of his siblings once remarked that a biography of Jack could be entitled *John Kennedy: A Medical History*. He suffered from colitis, urinary troubles, extreme back pain, malaria, prostatitis, Addison's disease, and other ailments. At the time, Addison's disease (a disorder of the adrenal glands that causes extreme weakness, low blood pressure, and discoloration of the skin) was still a potentially fatal malady.

The President had always been prone to illness. He nearly died of scarlet fever shortly before his third birthday, and had a difficult recovery from an appendicitis operation at 13. Rose

Kennedy remembered one of the children joking that "if a mosquito bit Jack Kennedy, the mosquito would die." In 1954, a staph infection brought on by a complex operation to insert a steel plate in his back nearly killed the senator. For the third time, he received last rites from a Catholic priest and recovered. As President, he frequently took steroids to fight the Addison's disease, and antispasmodics and painkillers for his back, as well as antibiotics, testosterone, sleeping pills, and a litany of other drugs. The more fragile he was, the more important it became to project an air of invincibility.

Because of the pain in his back, Kennedy sometimes took five showers a day. He sat in a rocking chair, which put less pressure on his lower back than normal chairs, and often resorted to wearing a back brace or using crutches. Despite the impression that he was very open with reporters, great efforts were made to conceal his illnesses and the extent to which they affected his life. Even after his death, his brother had the notes from his autopsy destroyed, and some of his doctors could never produce their files when the FBI requested them.

If the public had been aware of the quantity and severity of Kennedy's ailments, he likely never would have succeeded in becoming President. Since appearing healthy and physically fit was crucial to his campaign, Kennedy and his photographers produced pictures that reinforced the public perception of his virility. Because he was an active person by nature, and had grown up in a family that placed a high value on athletics, it was relatively easy to paint a picture of JFK as the model of youth and health.

In an interesting twist, it was because of his ailments that he took up the exercise regimen that he would be renowned for. White House physician George Burkley witnessed the deterioration of the President's back and his increased reliance on crutches and feared that he would be soon be confined to a wheelchair. When an orthopedic surgeon was brought in for a consultation, he insisted that injections and wearing braces without regular exercise therapy would not be enough to keep Jack walking. Thus, exercises in the White House gym and pool became part of the President's daily routine. He also received regular massages and heat therapy, and before long, getting away to the privacy of his gym regimen became a welcome breather for a man dealing with the stress of helming the country. To keep the details of his pitiable health private, he also insisted that his medical information be locked in a vault under the supervision of his secretary, Evelyn Lincoln.

In three years in office, the Kennedys faced struggles both at home and abroad, and each success and failure occurred in the open, on the front pages of newspapers, and to fanfare or criticism on the nightly news. To combat the negative stories coming out of the South and out of Vietnam, the Kennedys continued their goodwill tours around the world. Jackie's well-publicized visits to India and Pakistan offered brief respite from the Cold War tensions that weighed so heavily on the American people. Whether it was her choice of clothing fabrics to mirror the culture of the nations she visited, or her ability to speak an audience's language, the images of Jackie became ever more important. In these and other instances, the first family strove to pepper the tense news coverage with images that reflected their sophisticated, cultured, optimistic view of the world.

ON OCTOBER 23, 1962, NEWSPAPER HEADLINES ANNOUNCED THE CRISIS IN CUBA TO THE WORLD.

A WORLD IN CRISIS

Early into his administration Kennedy faced a near disaster, the failed Bay of Pigs invasion. Planned before he took office and executed with insufficient support, the mission failed, causing detractors to criticize the inexperienced President. Kennedy took to television to publicly take responsibility for the failed mission. Calling the Bay of Pigs incident a "tough kick in the leg," Kennedy knew that greater challenges lay ahead. After a difficult reception with Nikita Khrushchev in Vienna in June 1961, the first incarnation of the Berlin Wall arose in Soviet-controlled East Berlin that summer. Fears of an impending nuclear conflict rose. The world seemed to teeter on the brink of destruction.

ABOVE: *April 17, 1961. Former President Dwight D. Eisenhower and JFK meet at Camp David to discuss the failed Bay of Pigs invasion.*
LEFT: *August 1961. An early manifestation of the Berlin Wall*

HUGH SIDEY: It was a very scary time. People forget that now. There were four million people under arms in Eastern Europe. We had half that number. We had a margin in nuclear weapons but the Soviet Union also had nuclear weapons and had bigger rockets than we did. I went to the Oval Office one time after Kennedy's summit with Khrushchev and it was late and Kennedy said, "I think there will be a nuclear exchange." Sometimes he was just overwhelmed at the somber nature of what lay ahead. He said, "If I know anything about weaponry, going clear back to the bow and arrow, when it is invented, people build them and build them and somebody uses them." Bobby Kennedy told me that later that summer, in July of '61, things got grim. The Berlin Wall went up. They were up in the bedroom and they were talking about this terrible situation and he said, "You know, Bobby, it doesn't matter about you and me. We've had a good life. But it is just inconceivable to me that this could happen to innocent children." It was a tough world.

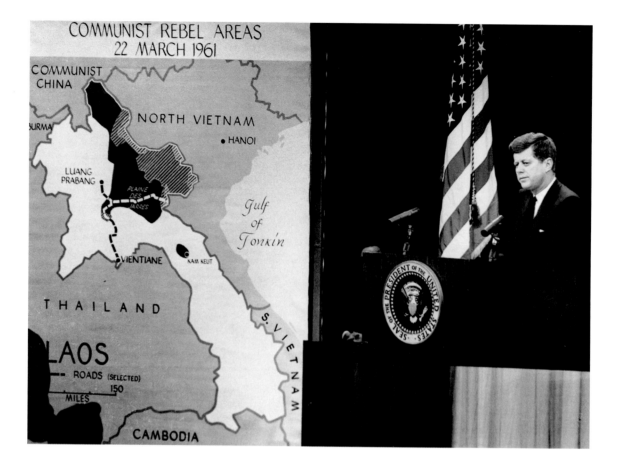

ROBERT DALLEK: U.S. involvement in Vietnam dramatically increased during Kennedy's thousand days. The roughly 800 military advisers Eisenhower had sent to Saigon grew to 16,700. It was a demonstration of Kennedy's reluctance to "lose" Vietnam. After the setbacks at the Bay of Pigs and in Vienna, he was eager to prevent another communist advance or what could be seen as a U.S. defeat. Yet at the same time, he was greatly concerned not to turn the conflict into an American war in which U.S. troops did the fighting for the South Vietnamese. A larger war in Southeast Asia had the potential to become another flash point in Soviet-American relations. Moreover, Kennedy feared that such a conflict could turn into another Korea, which drew in the Chinese and destroyed Truman's domestic political support. Consequently, in 1963 Kennedy began making plans to withdraw U.S. advisers. He was particularly concerned to ensure that U.S. reporters in Saigon did not turn the conflict into a front-page story that would embarrass the administration. There is reason to believe that Kennedy was planning to sharply reduce involvement in Vietnam after reelection in 1964.

LEFT: *March 22, 1961. President Kennedy addresses the growth of communism in Southeast Asia in a live televised press conference.*
ABOVE: *An American helicopter hovers above soldiers in Vietnam, 1962.*

CRISIS IN CUBA

In October 1962, Kennedy received the toughest news yet. U.S. planes had photographed nuclear missiles in Cuba. That the Soviet Union could position such deadly weapons less than 90 miles from the United States prompted an international crisis. For 13 days senior administration officials monitored the events in Cuba, weighing their options and hoping for a peaceful resolution. To display the United States's resolve, Kennedy ordered a quarantine of Soviet ships, and offered to remove U.S. missiles from Turkey if Khrushchev would remove his missiles from Cuba. On October 28 Khrushchev began removing the missiles, and the world breathed a sigh of relief.

LEFT: *Aerial photography of a Havana-bound shipload of warplanes stirred fear in the United States during the early days of the crisis.*
ABOVE: *October 22, 1962. President Kennedy announces the presence of Soviet missiles in Cuba to the nation.*

LETITIA BALDRIGE: The Cuban missile crisis turned the temperature down in Washington from a warm, brisk, vigorously paced atmosphere to a cold, marbleized mausoleum. All social activities were canceled. No one was allowed into the mansion. Staffers walked softly through the corridors. During this siege the President, with his nightly TV reports, helped comfort many, but worried many others who felt that in making these reports the President was telling us that things were far more serious than we realized.

ROBERT DALLEK: In October 1962, Kennedy faced the greatest test of his Presidency and the most dangerous crisis during the Cold War. Nikita Khrush-chev's decision to put Soviet missiles in Cuba, or what Kennedy accurately described as offensive weapons, brought Moscow and Washington to the brink of a nuclear war. Kennedy's military chiefs urged an aerial assault or an invasion of the island. Fearing that the Soviets might be able to launch some of their missiles against U.S. targets, which would then require a direct attack on Soviet territory, Kennedy decided to rely on a naval blockade, or quarantine as he called it, to persuade Moscow to remove the missiles from Cuba. Making clear to Khrushchev that he would use military power to prevent Moscow from establishing a missile base in the Caribbean, Kennedy forced Khrushchev to back down. During the crisis, Kennedy made his resolve clear to the public, which underscored for Khrushchev that Kennedy was determined to block what Americans saw as a Soviet act of aggression. Kennedy's success in the missile crisis heightened his domestic political appeal, ensured that he could win Senate approval for a limited nuclear test ban treaty in 1963, and made his reelection in 1964 a near certainty.

LEFT: *October 29, 1962. Kennedy meets with advisers during the Cuban missile crisis.*

ABOVE: *June 26, 1963. Kennedy prepares to addresses the crowd in Berlin.*
RIGHT: *August 5, 1963. Nikita Khrushchev announces the signing of the Nuclear Test Ban Treaty.*

MAKING HISTORY

When Nikita Khrushchev signed the Nuclear Test Ban Treaty in 1963, the world celebrated a small victory in the nuclear arms race. Kennedy considered the treaty an important first step in protecting the world from nuclear war. Earlier that year, in a speech in Berlin, Kennedy famously declared, "Ich bin ein Berliner—I am a Berliner," to a crowd of cheering admirers. These moments seem to reflect Kennedy at his best: a student of history, making history.

HUGH SIDEY: Kennedy fancied himself as out on the stage. With de Gaulle and Churchill and Stalin and Roosevelt. This is why he spoke the way he spoke. I stood below Kennedy in Berlin. His "Ich bin ein Berliner" speech was amazing. It just lifted you up. I could see it in his eyes. He was not just Jack Kennedy the former senator. He was out there playing the game. He was in the bosom of history—and he could feel that. You have to want to come out in history as a great man, and I think Kennedy understood that. But he also had the talent, he had the intellect, and he had the ability to absorb the material. Kennedy was out there on the horizon with Churchill, and that was his ideal. And we all loved that, I think. We like aristocracy when it is handled well.

LETITIA BALDRIGE: The John F. Kennedy I know wanted to be perceived as an intellectual, but also an aristocrat. Most would agree that he reached both goals. He was such a history buff, his greatest satisfaction, after his pride in his family, must have been knowing that he was living history, meeting this country's crises head-on and succeeding. He desperately wanted his legacy to be that he proved his ability to lead, to overcome disaster, but also to use the tremendous power he had just to make things better, every single day.

CRISIS AT HOME

While nuclear tension and the growing crisis in Vietnam threatened the United States from outside its borders, still more troubles threatened from within. During 1961 and 1962 the economy stalled despite the administration's best efforts to spur it along. In 1962, the price of steel caused another crisis, and Kennedy in consultation with his brother Robert successfully stood up to the challenge. And in the South, images of protesters fighting for civil rights were becoming hard to ignore. Kennedy had stepped in on civil rights on several occasions, but by 1963 the crisis was acute. That year, Martin Luther King led the famous March on Washington, and Kennedy brought his civil rights bill before Congress.

ABOVE: *April 1962. Labor Secretary Arthur Goldberg and George Meany, president of the AFL-CIO, discuss the steel crisis with Kennedy.*
RIGHT: *The President confers with brother and Attorney General Robert Kennedy during the steel crisis.*

ROBERT DALLEK: Although Kennedy now enjoys a reputation as a highly popular President, this was not always the case during his administration. A sluggish economy, bloodshed in Mississippi and Alabama over civil rights conflicts between blacks and white local authorities, and a failure to win legislative proposals for medical insurance for seniors, federal aid to elementary, secondary, and higher education, a tax cut, and civil rights undermined Kennedy's national appeal. A stymied domestic program raised doubts about Kennedy's effectiveness as a Chief Executive.

HUGH SIDEY: No two men were closer in the history of the Presidency than John and Robert Kennedy. The bond was forged by father Joe Kennedy, who told his children over and over that if they could count true friends outside their family on one hand, they would be lucky. Bobby never faltered as adviser, manager, strategist, and political muscleman in JFK's long rise up the ladder. Bobby either never entertained ambitions for himself or sublimated them as his brother marched on. No major issue came through the White House without having Bobby's fingerprints someplace.

ABOVE: *June 19, 1963. Kennedy meets with educators to discuss civil rights in the United States.*
RIGHT: *August 28, 1963. Martin Luther King leads the historic March on Washington.*

BARBARA BAKER BURROWS: For a President whose personal fortunes were so dependent on the camera, it was oddly appropriate that photographs should, quite literally, put right on his desktop the big issues of the day. In particular, the pictures that record the vicious implementation of Birmingham Police Commissioner Bull Connor's orders to disperse the protesters with fire hoses and dogs in the spring of 1963 were met with mass revulsion and outrage. Confronted with one photograph, Kennedy's immediate reaction was testy—his administration had sought to balance its commitment to civil rights with the political expediencies of the issue. Yet, barely a month later, calling it a "moral crisis," he addressed the nation and introduced legislation. Television coverage of the March on Washington later that summer gave another boost to the legislation that would become the Civil Rights Act of 1964.

HUGH SIDEY: Kennedy was at first not quite sure about the rising tide of civil rights. His scholarship and his experience had little to do with American blacks. The only part of the South he knew was the golden coast of Florida's Palm Beach, where his father had a mansion frequented by his son in his flamboyant bachelor days. True, Kennedy had watched the late dispatch of troops to Little Rock by Dwight Eisenhower in 1957. The young senator had muted criticism for the response because by 1957 he was running for the Presidency himself and paid little attention as the high school integration crisis faded out of the headlines. He was awakened during his own presidential campaign in 1960 when Martin Luther King was arrested for a sit-in and put in isolation in federal prison. From a campaign stop in Chicago he called Coretta Scott King, the prisoner's wife, offering his sympathy and any other help he could muster to pressure King's release, which occurred in a few days. In the White House he began to feel the full fury of black America in pursuit of equal rights and opportunities. He was more aware of "the black problem," but the Cold War still consumed most of his time. Kennedy and his White House changed in the spring of 1963 when Martin Luther King sponsored his huge protests in Birmingham, and Kennedy in the White House watched in horror, as did the entire nation, when Birmingham's Public Safety Commissioner Bull Connor unleashed snarling dogs and water cannon on the demonstrators. The visual impact of such racial malice changed this country as much as anything in that period. As the Kennedy brothers sat in the serenity of the White House watching the images flicker in front of them, they also changed and vowed to press for more civil rights.

ROBERT DALLEK: During the first two and half years of his Presidency, Kennedy was cautious about asking for civil rights legislation. True, he understood that this was a compelling issue that would not disappear. But he knew that he would not be able to push a conservative Congress dominated by southern Democrats into passing a major civil rights law. Instead, he used executive action to limit discrimination against African Americans. By the spring of 1963, however, the struggle by southern blacks, especially the Southern Christian Leadership Conference (SCLC), to gain admission to segregated state universities and eliminate segregation in other places of public accommodation forced Kennedy to respond. Repression of protesters engaged in passive resistance, particularly the use of force by southern white law enforcement officials, compelled the JFK Administration to act. Bull Connor in Birmingham, Alabama, was a symbol of southern brutality against blacks asking for equal rights. Television pictures of unprovoked attacks on demonstrators disturbed and angered Kennedy and decided him to press Congress for a comprehensive civil rights bill. A Kennedy speech in June 1963 requesting congressional action helped give him a reputation as a champion of equal rights and eclipsed impressions of him as too cautious on the need for a fundamental social change in American life.

LEFT: *Charles Evers, brother of murdered civil rights activist Medgar Evers, was elected mayor of Fayette, Mississippi, in 1969, the first black man to hold office in the state since Reconstruction. He sits beneath portraits of John F. Kennedy, Robert F. Kennedy, and Martin Luther King.*

MANAGING THE NEWS

In 1963 the term "photo op" had not yet been coined, but the idea was certainly familiar. Through photo ops and other means, the Kennedy Administration exercised a great amount of control over the press, achieved in part through the illusion of unprecedented access. Kennedy's administration allowed open access to all members of the staff, and Kennedy himself cultivated friendships with a number of reporters. This close relationship led some to criticize the way the administration "managed the news." Indeed, it is hard to believe that the administration was able to conceal the severity of the President's numerous ailments and his now legendary extramarital affairs. But in this pre-Watergate world, there was a level of trust and responsibility between the President and the press. Before Kennedy the President's personal life rarely made the news; the press had little precedent to cover scandal.

ABOVE: *October 24, 1962. The President conducts a live press conference to announce the strategic quarantine of Cuba.*
RIGHT: *Released by the White House at the President's request, this charming photo appeared in newspapers around the world.*

ABOVE: October 1960. An energetic Kennedy leaps out of his car to greet a Bronx, New York, bride during his campaign.
RIGHT: June 1, 1961. After straining his back in a tree-planting ceremony in Canada, Kennedy was forced to walk with crutches.

LETITIA BALDRIGE: There is no question that there was a spin on the President's health. He was a lot sicker than he appeared to be. But that is one of the reasons I admired him—he never let the pain show. He would just go limp after some of his appearances after being very "up" for the television crews. He would take a deep breath and you knew he was in terrible pain. He went on regardless. He never gave in to any of it. We had such admiration for him. He was such a trouper.

BARBARA BAKER BURROWS: Photographer Paul Schutzer routinely witnessed the Kennedy who jumped from cars and passed for touchdowns. Because of pictures like his, it was a young, active President that America came to know. Yet the country had also heard about his pain, how Profiles in Courage had been written between two spinal operations, and it knew about the relief he found in a rocking chair. But the photographs told another story, sometimes even when they didn't. When, for example, we saw in a picture a curious President devouring the newspapers, we missed a man strategically leaning to relieve his pain.

HUGH SIDEY: Perhaps because we were so swept along by his vitality and the newness of his politics we probably didn't pay enough attention to his illness. Maybe we should have dug deeper into that. But we didn't do that in those days. We knew about his back, but it didn't seem to cripple him. He was out campaigning from five in the morning till midnight. This was no invalid. This was a guy out there all the time, and we had fun with him. He was irreverent and he had good humor and his message was middle of the road—a lot of people say liberal, but not by today's standards. He was tough on defense. He was for social programs to ease poverty. And he was up in the forefront on civil rights. Perhaps not as much as some wanted, but I think he reflected America. So we journalists took him into our own group. Perhaps too much. When I first began covering the White House there were a dozen of us in the press corps. Maybe there were 20 if the news was big. Today there are 50 or 100, or on a big day 200 or 300. There are cameras up all the time. It's a 24-hour news cycle. Television demands a mini-drama every night on the news. Of course print followed suit, and we added people to the White House beat—and it became far more intensive and intrusive. And I think that out of self-defense presidential candidates had to withdraw. I think it is a hard call to judge which came first—the defensive nature of the candidate or this clamoring horde of newspeople that would never let up. I think the sins are on both sides.

ROBERT DALLEK: Kennedy was one of a handful of modern Presidents who effectively managed his relations with the media. This is not to suggest that there weren't tensions with journalists and publishers. When the *New York Herald Tribune* criticized him for his actions toward steel companies, Kennedy canceled the White House subscription. He also tried unsuccessfully to persuade the *New York Times* to replace David Halberstam in Saigon with a less critical correspondent. His actions provoked complaints about administration efforts to manage the news. Kennedy's frequent live news conferences, in which he showed a mastery of current events and a talent for responding thoughtfully to press queries, gave him a hold on journalists that exceeded anything Eisenhower and Nixon had achieved.

Kennedy projected an image of youthful energy that belied the reality of his physical condition. A reputation for athleticism added to the press and public view of him as a dynamic young President whose robust health gave him the wherewithal to shoulder the physical and psychological burdens of being President. The truth was more complicated. From childhood, Kennedy had suffered from spastic colitis, a life-threatening disease that doctors began treating with steroids in 1937, when the drugs first became available. The medicine contributed to the onset of Addison's disease, the impairment of his adrenal glands that made him dependent on cortisone throughout his Presidency. The steroids also caused osteoporosis of the lumbar spine and the terrible back problems he struggled with most of his life. Although his medical problems had no decisive impact on his functioning in the White House, they posed risks that were hidden from the public and might have cost him the 1960 election if they were well known.

LEFT: *Kennedy is pictured in one of his many rocking chairs, which helped ease his strained back.*
PREVIOUS PAGES: *Temporarily relieving his back pain, the president leans on a desk for support as he scans the papers.*

CHAPTER 6

Frozen in Time

President Kennedy went to Dallas in November 1963 to lay the groundwork for his reelection campaign. Kennedy's appeal was lost on much of the state. Even though he chose a popular Texas senator for his running mate, he had barely eked out a win there in 1960. If he hoped to carry Texas in 1964, he would need to spend more time in the Lone Star State. Much to their host's pleasure, Jackie decided to join him on this particular trip.

Trouble in the Democratic Party complicated planning for the trip. Texas Governor John Connally was up for reelection the next year, and was not keen on appearing to be too friendly with the first family. Further, there was a growing conservative/liberal rift within the party, and Vice President Johnson did not want to make it worse by appearing to favor either side. Jackie was always a huge hit with the crowds, and her presence may have softened some of the political rivalries that formed the background of the trip. President Kennedy saw the political squabbling and suspicious populace as a challenge, and the challenge excited him. He relished convincing Texans that he was their man and connecting with his fans outside of Washington, who always greeted him with more genuine enthusiasm than the ones inside the Beltway.

On the morning of November 22, the President and First Lady arrived in Dallas from Fort Worth shortly after 11:30 a.m. From the airport, they were scheduled to travel by motorcade with Governor Connally and his wife, Nellie, to a luncheon for 2,600 people at the Dallas Trade Mart. Lyndon and Lady Bird Johnson would ride in a second convertible. It was a beautiful November day, sunny and warm in Dallas, which began like any other for a President seeking reelection. As the motorcade turned west on Elm Street into Dealey Plaza, shots rang out. The President was hit twice, once in the neck and once in the back of his head. Governor Connally was also injured in the attack. Secret Service agents converged on the President's car, which then sped to the nearest hospital. The President's motionless body was admitted to Parkland Hospital at 1:38 p.m. where he was given last rites for the fourth and final time.

On the CBS television network, Walter Cronkite broke into the regularly scheduled soap opera, *As The World Turns*, with the chilling news: "In Dallas, Texas, three shots were fired at President Kennedy's motorcade. John F. Kennedy was declared dead at 2:00 p.m."

Jackie refused to change her blood-spattered Chanel suit for the dreary flight back to Washington. When Lady Bird Johnson gingerly suggested that she might feel a bit better in another outfit, Jackie replied, "I want them to see what they have done to Jack." In the famous image of Lyndon Johnson's swearing-in aboard Air Force One, Cecil Stoughton reportedly tried to frame the photo in such a way that the least amount of blood was visible. The press was waiting on the tarmac when the plane arrived at Andrews Air Force Base, and as Jackie intended, her bloodied clothes were an immediate reminder of the violence that had just ended an era and stolen a President and celebrity from his fans and his country.

November 22, 1963, is among the most poignant historical milestones in the American consciousness. Anyone who lived through that fateful day can recall with lucidity where they were and what they were doing. For many Americans, Kennedy's death marked a turning point in this country's history. The heart-wrenching images of Jackie in her bloodstained suit and of three-year-old John saluting his fallen father have become icons of the loss of idealism suffered that

LEFT: *November 22, 1963. A warm welcome greeted the President and First Lady upon their arrival at Dallas's Love Field.*
PREVIOUS PAGES: *November 21, 1963. JFK shakes hands with well-wishers in Fort Worth, Texas.*

day—a loss of innocence that many argue has never been regained.

Like so much else in Kennedy's life, his assassination was captured on film. That the dashing "prince in his prime" had been struck down dominated the press, both international and nationwide for weeks on end, and the Abraham Zapruder film—a silent, 8-mm, home-movie record of the Kennedy motorcade shot just before, during, and immediately after the shooting—is still replayed and dissected to this day.

Word of the President's death traveled quickly around the country and around the world. Crowds gathered in front of electronics store windows to catch the news. Every head was buried in the paper, in desperate search for answers. A Moscow newscaster burst into tears on camera; French President Charles de Gaulle reported, "They are crying all over France. It is as though he were a Frenchman, a member of their own family." Flags were lowered to half-mast in Indonesia. Sékou Touré, president of the West African nation of Guinea, announced that he "lost [my] only true friend in the outside world" and explained that his country "seemed to have fallen under the spell of the courageous young hero of far away, the slayer of dragons of discrimination, poverty, ignorance, and war." It is said that even Nikita Khrushchev, with whom Kennedy had clashed so many times, cried at the news of his tragic demise.

WALTER CRONKITE REMOVES HIS GLASSES AS HE ANNOUNCES THE PRESIDENT'S DEATH.

In the days after the assassination the President's young widow agreed to meet with writer Theodore White and speak about the President's death. The First Lady spoke about the meaning of history. "For a while I thought history was something that bitter old men wrote. But then I realized history made Jack what he was," she told the reporter. " You must think of him as this little boy, sick so much of the time, reading in bed, reading history, reading the Knights of the Round Table, reading Marlborough. For Jack, history was full of heroes." It was during this conversation that she mentioned the President's favorite song, from a popular musical of the time. White's epilogue to the President made the most of her allusion to the idyllic life she shared with Jack. The song was "Camelot," from the Broadway play of the same name. The song contained the words "Let it never be forgot, that once there was a spot, for one brief shining moment that was known as Camelot." The words struck an instantaneous chord with the grieving nation. Despite later attempts to play down its significance, the idea of "Camelot" crystallized an era, and forever after the Kennedy years have been referred to as "Camelot."

Scores of conspiracy theories have been offered up to explain the assassination. They star pro-Castro Cubans, anti-Castro Cubans, mobsters, communists bent on world domination, oil tycoons bent on world domination, vengeful allies of South Vietnam's former first lady, Madame Nhu, over-ambitious Lyndon Johnson supporters, the CIA, the FBI, double agents, triple agents, and any number of mystery assassins on the grassy knoll. Although some were discredited immediately, others have been carefully considered over the years. Each frame of the Zapruder film has been scrutinized, as has every angle leading to the President and Governor Connally. Every detail of Lee Harvey Oswald's and Jack Ruby's lives has been picked over in an attempt to explain why Kennedy met his untimely death.

Certainly the assassination plays a huge part in the myth of Kennedy, but there are other components that add to the outpouring of interest that continues to this day. That Kennedy had not fulfilled many of his aims tops the list. As *Washington Post* editor and Kennedy friend Ben Bradlee put it, "When he died, most of his appeal was promise. He hadn't delivered all that much in terms of changing the country except in that sense of excitement and hope. But you know that's all on the come, all to be, and he never got there."

Kennedy exuded a familiarity that let the public feel close to him. And the photographic record that he left behind is a perpetual invitation for new generations of spectators to feel that intimacy with John Kennedy and his family. Hugh Sidey described this particular tragedy as threefold: "First off, a friend's killed … I think America felt that…. Then, secondly, a President, the head of our government. He's cut off. He's dead. It's over with. And then thirdly, an administration,

a new frontier, is gone, because that's a very personal thing. The tone and the style of any administration comes from the President. And that was gone instantly."

The sadness, shock, and fear throughout the country was also caught on film in the bewildering days that followed the assassination—on the faces of strangers as well as friends, family, and acquaintances of the fallen President. Then, three days later, the funeral was televised, giving the world even more iconic memories of the Kennedys—of John Jr. saluting his father's casket, and Jackie walking determinedly under her veil.

The televised funeral, with its many millions of viewers, allowed a far greater portion of the population to feel a part of the tragedy. The assassination of Abraham Lincoln and the death of Franklin Roosevelt, both of whom had been a part of the American landscape for so long at the time their deaths, were both extraordinarily traumatizing events. Both occurred at times when the country was still plagued by wartime wounds (FDR did not live to see the end of World War II). And yet their deaths did not inspire the mythology that Kennedy's did.

One could argue that the assassination did more to increase television's role in politics than even the Kennedy-Nixon debates. And the focus remained on the Kennedys even after Jack's death. Bobby and Teddy were still in Washington. And a few short years later, Bobby

LYNDON JOHNSON TAKES THE
OATH OF OFFICE ABOARD AIR
FORCE ONE ON THE RETURN
TO WASHINGTON.

would also announce his candidacy for the Presidency. He too would be assassinated. Jackie would be followed by the paparazzi and would remain a top draw of newspapers and magazines for the rest of her life, despite her desire to remain private.

In 1960, when Kennedy assumed the presidential mantle, roughly a dozen reporters covered regular briefings. Perhaps 20 would attend a more newsworthy day. Today, those numbers are more like 50 to 100 reporters on a quiet day, and more on a "big news" day. Kennedy's presidency occupied a unique time when televisions' influence loomed large, but in general, reporters asked respectful questions and did not pry into public leaders' personal lives. Most reporters also left the editorializing to the columnists and editorial pages.

Today's cat-and-mouse game between the press and the Presidency seems unimaginable when we hear of Kennedys camaraderie with reporters. These were men who conducted interviews while sailing aboard the *Honey Fitz* or even while skinny-dipping. By inviting the press into his home and introducing them to his children or conducting one-on-one interviews and asking publishers' opinions, Kennedy encouraged the media's insatiable hunger for insider access to the lives of our elected leaders. President Kennedy set the stage for the media frenzies we witness today, and politicians like Richard Nixon and Bill Clinton would pay the price in years to come.

The public hunger for news about President Kennedy and his family increased the public's interest in constant news from the Oval Office and sped up television's reliance on news from the White House. The increased interest in the President, and the hurt caused by revelations of Kennedy's shortcomings, also helped to create an environment where only a select few people could

THE SHOCKING NEWS OF THE PRESIDENT'S DEATH MADE HEADLINES AROUND THE WORLD.

ever hope to occupy the office of President of the United States. John Kennedy won the election despite his many illnesses and his reckless philandering, something that is no longer possible given today's aggressive media climate. And the public reaction to learning they'd been duped was mixed and intense: Some people pointedly refused to have his name slandered by the truth; and others felt betrayed. They were angry, saddened, and above all, each new revelation added to the mistrust of the government and the media, helping public perception climb toward its current, negative plateau.

That the Zapruder film was not screened publicly until 1975 is telling. In 1963, it would have been considered too violent, too gory, and too early for the emotionally wrought public. Twelve years later, the film was televised on ABC and CBS. At that point, it had been more than ten years since television audiences had witnessed water cannon and Bull Conner's police dogs unleashed on civil rights demonstrators in Birmingham. And television coverage brought gory images of Vietnam into people's homes night after night. After so much bloodshed, and the assassinations of so many great leaders, the public was far more ready to see the historic murder that had so dramatically changed the course of American history.

In truth, the myth of Camelot is at odds with much that is now known about President Kennedy. But the Kennedys were the first political family with real media savvy, and they used it efficiently. The roots of the Kennedy political dynasty were firmly planted by Joseph Kennedy, the patriarch of an immigrant family that reached the nation's highest office within three generations. But it was John Kennedy's ability to befriend the media that kept the press, in part, from revealing his less stellar sides. Hugh Sidey put it best when he said, "Let's be honest about it, we probably violated the rules of journalism as set down in the classroom. We liked the guy. Just plainly and simply, we liked the guy. He liked us."

Whether it was conservative 1960s protocol that protected the President's secrets or this particular politician's charisma and cooperation with the press that kept his scandals from the front pages, he was the last in his line to enjoy such a relationship with the media. Perhaps the many crises and foreign policy matters kept reporters too busy to attack the President's personal life, but it is safe to assume that in today's media climate, while a dire foreign crisis might bump a tawdry sexual indiscretion or hidden illness off the front page, those stories would still make the papers.

Rising to power in front of the camera—and dying before it as well—made John F. Kennedy immortal. More than 40 years after his death, most photos reveal a dashing, handsome man—a hero with no hint of frailty or illness. And his appearance in these iconic images is how he will remain in American popular memory: the vigorous young president who never reached age 47. Despite his terrible heath problems—his bouts with colitis, complications from the steroids prescribed for his digestive disorders, and progressive back problems, he remains in everlasting images an athletic-looking man. Like Woodrow Wilson and Franklin D. Roosevelt before him, Kennedy was spared public scrutiny of his frailties and illnesses. His photographers neglected to capture photos of the crutches in his Senate chamber, or of the President looking wan and ill, both because access to him was cleverly controlled when he was ill, and

FOR DAYS AND YEARS AFTER THE ASSASSINATION, INTIMATES AND HISTORIANS WOULD SEEK TO EXPLAIN THE UNIQUENESS OF THE ERA.

because of the shared knowledge about the importance of youth and vigor in the President. His successful media management during his lifetime has perpetuated the desired mythology about him to this day.

The Kennedy era helped to usher in the modern age of celebrity, in which spectators demand constant access to high-profile people. As much as the media helped the President, it also created intense pressure for an administration whose successes and failures were scrutinized daily. Housewives in the 1960s wanted to know what shampoo or skin-care regimen Jackie used and who the Kennedys had for dinner, and these prying impulses have only intensified—certainly to the point that anyone with the sexual and medical track record of John F. Kennedy would never again be able to slip into the White House without his foibles being detected and dissected.

Historian and social commentator Daniel Boorstin wrote, "Nothing is really real to us unless it happens on television." Since Kennedy made sure that cameras trailed him and constantly caught his "good side," he made sure his most positive attributes (whether or not they were true) were the ones accepted as real. This is one of the instances where the truth is juicier than the stories being told. And he has continued to captivate audiences; whether it was the 1963 film rendition of his PT-109 experience, the 1991 Oliver Stone film JFK, or Robert Dallek's 2003 best-seller An Unfinished Life, Kennedy was and is a draw in the cinema and the bookstore. Jack Kennedy, his family, and those who aided in his image-making, did their jobs so expertly that the myths, stories, and controversies about the 35th President thrive to this day—and a wealth of photos, recordings, films, books, and anecdotes ensure that the Kennedy mystique will live on.

NOVEMBER 22, 1963

The events of November 22, 1963, are indelibly etched into our national consciousness. Arriving in Dallas with his sights on reelection, the President embarked on a whirlwind two-day schedule of speeches and receptions. All was going as planned as the President's motorcade sped toward Dallas's Dealey Plaza in the early afternoon of November 22. Thousands of Dallas residents lined the streets to welcome the President and First Lady to their town. And then three shots rang out. From the Dallas Book Depository an assassin's bullets stopped the motorcade and ended a bright chapter of American history. Over the next three days the world would come together as never before to watch the news of the assassination and funeral on television, and collectively mourn for a lost vision of America.

ABOVE: *November 22, 1963. The President and Mrs. Kennedy smile and wave at crowds lining the motorcade route in Dallas.*

LEFT: *This overhead view of Dealey Plaza shows the area as it appeared on November 22, 1963.*

ROBERT DALLEK: Kennedy went to Dallas, Texas, to burnish his image in a state that seemed at political risk in a 1964 campaign. His civil rights proposal was a particular problem across the entire South. Democratic Party feuding between liberal and conservative factions also made the state vulnerable to the Republicans. Kennedy's visit was an effort to bring the warring factions together and shore up his popularity among voters. Warnings that the city was a hotbed of right-wing sentiment and that he might meet violent opposition did not deter him from the visit.

HUGH SIDEY: Dallas was sunny, bright, and as far as we could tell, happy. People six deep lined the streets. We thought there might be a few protesters chanting, a placard or two insulting the visitor. Standard fare for such a conservative neighborhood. Not a sign out there. Reporters in the first press bus lounged and joked and considered it a routine campaign swing, warm-up for 1964. Then came the three reports, noises—could they be shots? The reporters jolted upright, then dismissed any thought of trouble, settled back for another second until the chaos of the grassy knoll became apparent.

BARBARA BAKER BURROWS: If photographs had helped define the Kennedy presidency, it was to be no different on its final day. But like the cacophony of news reports that filled the air, the pictures would take some editing. A few would become icons. One—Cecil Stoughton's reassuring record of LBJ's swearing-in—would be taken with the specific purpose of securing the United States.

Mrs. Kennedy too had a point to make. She chose not to change the pink suit in which she had started the day. Now stained with her husband's blood as she accompanied him home, it shouted her accusation of crimes we had not yet seen.

Although remarkable from our camera-obsessed perspective, the President's body was back in Washington and the only pictures of the shooting had yet to be seen. It was not until the next morning that *Life*'s Richard Stolley would view them, actually seven seconds of film, with Abraham Zapruder operating the projector. Stolley had got there first, and with the magazine's deep pockets and reputation behind him—and competing journalists in the next room—the two men reached a deal. It depended as much on its guarantees that the pictures would not be sensationalized as on money. The first few small frames were published in black and white 3 days later; the weekly magazine would not run them larger and in color for another three years. The film was not shown.

What the public did see over the next few days was an assassin shot, and those vignettes—a girl's gloved hand on her father's coffin, a widow's veil, a riderless horse, and a son's salute—such a fitting end to Camelot.

With Kennedy's death, television crossed an important threshold, moving closer to the role it has today as the prime provider of news. The memories, even those recorded on 8-mm film, remain frozen—a series of stills.

ROBERT DALLEK: Kennedy's assassination was a terrible blow to the nation. The country prided itself on its nonviolent politics. The assassination made America seem like an unstable banana republic. This was especially galling in a time when Americans liked to compare their representative system of government with repressive communist rule that tolerated no dissent from a party line.

The country could not understand why anyone would want to kill someone as appealing and successful as Kennedy. It could not accept that the killing was the act of a single individual—Lee Harvey Oswald. Instead, a large majority of Americans believed that there was a conspiracy at work, which they hoped in time would come to light. The most immediate reaction to the killing was a national outpouring of grief, which for the first time in the country's history was played out on television. The funeral procession, which was attended by leaders from all over the world, was indelibly printed on people's minds by the TV cameras that recorded every minute of the service. Like Pearl Harbor, Franklin Roosevelt's death, and now 9/11, the Kennedy assassination and funeral are part of the shared national experience.

ABOVE: *November 22, 1963. A hastily abandoned bouquet rests on the seat of the convertible that had been carrying Lyndon Johnson.*
PREVIOUS PAGES: *November 22, 1963. Dallas clothing manufacturer Abraham Zapruder captured the shooting on his 8-mm home-movie camera.*

BARBARA BAKER BURROWS: In a long career filled with remarkable work, if Carl Mydans had a signature photograph, it would show Gen. Douglas MacArthur honoring his pledge to return to the Philippines, wading ashore in 1945. Carl had lived in Asia, and in fact, so much of his career had been spent abroad that he was one of the few *Life* photographers with little association with the Kennedys. He was in the United States on November 22, 1963, but out of the New York office. "You're the last one," he was told when he reported in that evening. His vague assignment: "Go out somewhere, and bring something back." After a few unsatisfying frames taken around the city, on impulse, he boarded a train from Grand Central, destination unknown. Well removed from Washington and 1,500 miles from Dallas, Carl's photograph, taken on that train, told everything of a shocked nation absorbed by the President's assassination.

LEFT: *November 23, 1963. Riders on a New York train read the news of the assassination.*

A NATION MOURNS

After lying in state for 24 hours in the East Room of the White House, the President's coffin was moved to the U.S. Capitol on Sunday, November 24, where it was placed on the same catafalque that had held Abraham Lincoln. More than 250,000 mourners streamed through the building to pay their respects. The solemnity of the hours was interrupted by further developments in the unfolding drama: As television cameras covered the transfer of Lee Harvey Oswald to a nearby jail on Sunday morning, Dallas nightclub owner Jack Ruby shot and killed the President's assassin.

ABOVE: *November 24, 1963. Jacqueline and Caroline Kennedy kneel at the casket during the Capitol Rotunda ceremony.*
RIGHT: *November 24, 1963. More than 250,000 mourners paid their respects as the President lay in state at the Capitol.*

HUGH SIDEY: We should have known it was coming, but we did not; the worldwide gasp of horror at Kennedy's death was beyond any calculation. We had followed him overseas and all over America, and we had seen the outpouring of affection for him and for Jackie, whether at the Berlin Wall or along the squalid streets in Mexico. We did not realize the power of our own craft. Because we were racing to keep up at the center of this youthful caravan, we did not figure how the intimate images of the Kennedys at work and play and now on hundreds of millions of television screens had permeated the globe from mud hut to palace. The tragedy in Dallas and its aftermath became the first nonstop television reality show, running for three solid days. He was in myth and rising.

LETITIA BALDRIGE: The international sadness felt at the loss of John F. Kennedy was simply immeasurable. Foreigners would stop Americans on the streets, in order to say in their own way and language, "I'm so sorry for your loss." A beautiful young President, with a beautiful young wife and two perfect children—what world leaders could ever take their places? The answer was they couldn't, probably not in this century or the next. Jacqueline Kennedy taught the world to mourn with the utmost dignity and grace. She went through all the formal protocol of a state funeral, a heavy black veil covering her face, maintaining her composure. Her personal grief became everyone's grief.

ABOVE: *Flanked by Robert Kennedy and Edward Kennedy, Mrs. Kennedy walked behind her husband's coffin from the White House to St. Matthew's Cathedral.*

LEFT: *November 25, 1963. Jackie, John Jr., and Caroline stand on the steps of the White House before the funeral procession begins.*

HUGH SIDEY: Yet another myth developed within the larger Kennedy myth, and that was that Jackie had instantly recognized she must give her husband the most glorious tribute and moving burial since that of Abraham Lincoln, and that she had given orders that the Lincoln rituals were to be researched and followed in detail. That never happened. Waiting at the Bethesda Naval Hospital as the autopsy proceeded, Jackie had been told gently by Bobby that they would have to think of what they were going to do for Jack's services once the horrible night was over. "It's in the guide-book," Jackie responded. She referred to the White House Historical Association's tourist guide, which had been edited by her and included an engraving of Lincoln's body on its catafalque. That is all it took. The Lincoln model was on everybody's mind, and it all fell into place as staff and friends rushed off to follow this slender but perfectly logical lead. A call from Bobby and the actual Lincoln catafalque was found and rushed into place. Historian Arthur Schlesinger, Jr., routed out an expert on the Lincoln rites from the Library of Congress, and near midnight was poking through old files by flashlight for century-old accounts of the service in the press. But Jackie's ideas went far beyond Lincoln. She detailed her touches for the ceremonies: an honor guard from the Special Forces, the old military tradition of the riderless horse, the walk of the heads of state to St. Matthew's Cathedral for last rites, burial in Arlington Cemetery on a hill overlooking Washington and beneath an eternal flame. This was the framework from Jackie's mind—history, pageantry, faith, family, patriotism. The rest was up to the massive assemblage of media that had descended from all over the world. Not since Franklin Roosevelt's death had the nation paused so long to mourn in such grand style.

LETITIA BALDRIGE: It had been Jackie's decision to carry out the protocol of Abraham Lincoln's funeral for her husband. Since no one would deny her anything at this point, the military worked long and hard to find the description of that assassinated President's funeral. The plan was rigorously replicated. The flag-covered coffin was stationed in the East Room for a viewing for close friends, Cabinet members, and family. Then came the walk to St. Matthew's for the religious service, followed by the somber journey of accompanying the flag-covered caisson from the cathedral to its resting place in Arlington National Cemetery. An eternal flame was lit to mark the site permanently for all to see. The horses had been specially trained to pull the caisson to the burial site across the Potomac River. None of the massive crowds of bystanders missed the symbolism of the military boot turned backward on the empty saddle of the black horse as it moved through the throngs lining the route. The boot was the symbol of a hero who had died in battle. The nation watched in awe as television captured the pageantry. The prayers over the grave, the salute with rifles, the firing of the 21 guns, the folding 13 times of the flag taken from the top of the casket into a compact triangle, and the handing of it the widow—all standard operating procedure for the highest forms of military funeral services. Because of John F. Kennedy's assassination, many nations of the free world went into national mourning. The people of those countries understood the importance of this moment in history. They had all been present— thanks to television.

RIGHT: *November 25, 1963. The funeral procession crosses Memorial Bridge as it makes its way toward Arlington Cemetery.*
FOLLOWING PAGES: *November 25, 1963. Jacqueline Kennedy receives the flag that was draped over the President's coffin.*

THE WORLD
MOURNS

From London's Westminster Abbey to the Kremlin, mourners around the world paid tribute to President Kennedy. The bell in Westminster Cathedral tolled for an hour—a tribute typically reserved for royalty. Mourners gathered in Berlin for a torchlight march to City Hall, where the President had delivered a rousing speech not even six months before. Igor Stravinsky conducted a choral tribute in a Roman church. Around the world mourners shared the grief of the United States, and honored the fallen President.

ABOVE: *November 25, 1963. Londoners gather to pray for John F. Kennedy in Westminster Cathedral.*
RIGHT: *The audience at the State Opera House in Munich, Germany, stands to observe a moment of silence for Kennedy.*

ROBERT DALLEK: Kennedy's funeral temporarily bound Americans together and created a fund of sympathy for the country around the globe. In some peculiar way, it made Kennedy into an enduring hero who continues to be seen as a great President. Had Kennedy lived, won a second term, and served for eight years, it is doubtful that he would be remembered as fondly as he is now. As with all Presidents, the limitations of his Presidency would be a part of his legacy and that would diminish his current standing. Because he died after only a thousand days in office, his Presidency remains a kind of blank slate which historians and the public can fill in as they choose.

HUGH SIDEY: Yes, there was a Camelot. Those of us who lived it will argue with the scoffers. Maybe a term from a Broadway musical with its fairy-tale lyrics invites derision, but when you were on the ground in this army of young idealists in a nation which stood astride the world and had a heart for what is right, it was not much of a stretch in those heady days to hum—and to believe—"Let it never be forgot, that once there was a fleeting wisp of glory called Camelot." It is traditional wisdom that each new generation of chroniclers scorns the previous generation, has doubts about the future, and raises its own times and struggles as glamorous and virtuous. FDR's New Dealers and Truman's Fair Dealers were still very much around the capital when Kennedy rose to power, and they were deeply suspicious of the new elegance and youthful enthusiasts, and often dismissed them as spoiled and dreamy kids. But even within their aging ranks there were those who confessed when Kennedy was long swept into history there had been something different about his New Frontier. Maybe it was the following of writers and scholars, who in unprecedented numbers turned to political writing in his time and then mined the Kennedy memories, who helped fix the idea that these were golden years in the nation's life. Their style and eloquence made their adventures beyond imagination, and when played back in America had even greater impact. And there was danger in the world, which deepens and colors any story. The Cold War was at its height, and as John Kennedy grappled with each new crisis in the hair-trigger nuclear age, the vast majority of people prayed for his success and put him on a pedestal far above themselves.

LETITIA BALDRIGE: If the Kennedys had not been beautiful, if they had not been glamorous, if they had not given the best parties that were ever held in the White House, if Jackie hadn't been the chicest First Lady; if they hadn't had the cutest children, this legend would not have continued the way it did. If you put all of these factors together—the style and the grace and the beauty—you realize that the legend does continue, just as it does with Marilyn Monroe, or Greta Garbo, or anyone who was famous and has left us. I am very emotional about the White House, my White House. I wanted it to stay forever the way it was—so perfect and beautiful. But it will always be different from what it was in the Kennedy era. We cannot go back to that again. It is just like a door has closed and it will never be opened again.

RIGHT: *December 6, 1963. Jackie, John, and Caroline walk through the Rose Garden as they leave the White House.*

ROBERT DALLEK: Kennedy still has a continuing, powerful hold on the public's imagination. He was assassinated, and being martyred gave him a special place in presidential history. William McKinley was assassinated in 1901—he was also a popular President, elected to his second term. But 40 years after his death hardly anyone remembered him. By contrast, Kennedy continues to have an exceptional hold on the public. A lot of this has to do with television, which has frozen Kennedy in our minds at the age of 46. But there is something more at work here than just television or the assassination. Kennedy was the embodiment of hope for our country—of promise, of youth—a potential that was snuffed out. He spoke of a new frontier, of an alliance for progress, of putting a man on the moon by the end of the decade. Everything about him bespoke the best in America— our idealism, our hopes, our dreams—and people cling to that. Some people believe that 50 to 100 years from now Kennedy will fade out. He will be like one of those late-19th-century Presidents no one can remember. I doubt it. I think Kennedy will continue to have this exceptional hold on the public because he is associated with hope of a better future, as was his brother Robert, who was assassinated in 1968. The brothers were so full of promise. We associate them with a better America. We are all optimists, we want to believe that there will be progress, and we see Kennedy as embodying American idealism.

BARBARA BAKER BURROWS: For all the might-have-beens—another year, another term, a long and healthy life—we can never know where each would have led. Nor will we ever know what a modern-style media would have made of the Kennedys, even if the details of their lives remained unchanged. The record we do have is extensive. We have the photographs—oh, what photographs. And we have our memories.

For most of us now, when we think of the Kennedys, we still have at their center the President and First Lady, but theirs was a time before a substantial majority of today's Americans were born. Just as to an earlier generation the Kennedys were Joseph and Rose, so to new generations of Americans many new Kennedys have become known, and with them has come the telling and retelling of the stories of a charmed time. Sad still that ours was a tale of idealism, not defeated by failure, but run out of time. In *Profiles in Courage*, a young John Kennedy, who had already shown wartime bravery, wrote of "The courage of life"—"Often a less dramatic spectacle than the courage of a final moment; but it is no less a magnificent mixture of triumph and tragedy." All families experience triumph and tragedy, few as publicly or perhaps on the scale of the Kennedys, but for as long as their story can be told, there is every reason to believe the mystique will endure.

LEFT: *At his grave in Arlington Cemetery, an eternal flame burns in honor of President John F. Kennedy.*

INDEX

ACKNOWLEDGMENTS

National Geographic would like to thank Hugh Sidey, Letitia Baldrige, Barbara Baker Burrows, and Robert Dallek for their hard work and thoughtful contributions to this project. Special thanks go to Sarah Parvis, whose research, writing and editing skills were indispensable in helping to craft the essays for this book. James B. Hill and Colleen Cooney at the John F. Kennedy Library and Michelle Franklin, the Time-Life Researcher for Getty Images provided a great deal of help with photographic research. Leslie Kramer of Partisan Pictures and Dana Chivvis of National Geographic provided valuable photo research assistance. Jane Sunderland and Johnna Rizzo proofread the text. This book would not have been possible without the inspired work of Tracey Barry, who produced *The Kennedy Mystique*, the film on which this book is based.

PICTURE CREDITS

Key
JFKL = John F. Kennedy Presidential Library and Museum, Boston
TLP = Time Life Pictures
WHHA = White House Historical Association

Front Jacket, Hy Peskin/TLP/Getty Images
Spine, Arnold Newman/Getty Images
Back Jacket, Stanley Tretick/Sygma/CORBIS

2-3 & 4, Cecil Stoughton, White House/JFKL; 6, Bettmann/CORBIS; 8, Cornell Capa C/Magnum Photos; 10, Cecil Stoughton, White House, courtesy Hugh Sidey; 11, JFKL; 12, Cornell Capa C/Magnum Photos; 14, © Estate of Jacques Lowe/Woodfin Camp; 16, John F. Kennedy Library Foundation; 17, Bettmann/CORBIS; 19, Howard Sochurek/TLP/Getty Images; 20 (upper), JFKL; 20 (lower), Bettmann/CORBIS; 21, Keystone/Getty Images; 22-25 (all) JFKL; 26, Arnold Newman/Getty Images; 27 Yale Joel/TLP/Getty Images; 28, Condé Nast Archive/CORBIS; 29, Bettmann/CORBIS; 30, CBS/Landov; 31, Orlando Suero, Lowenherz Collection of Kennedy Photographs, Archives of the Peabody Institute of the Johns Hopkins University, Baltimore; 32-33, JFKL; 34 & 35, Ted Spiegel/CORBIS; 36 & 37, © Estate of Jacques Lowe/Woodfin Camp; 38, Hank Walker/TLP/Getty Images; 39-41 (all), © Estate of Jacques Lowe/Woodfin Camp; 42-43, Ralph Crane/TLP/Getty Images; 44, Stan Wayman/TLP/Getty Images; 45, © Estate of Jacques Lowe/Woodfin Camp; 46-47, Paul Schutzer/TLP/Getty Images; 49, Bettmann/CORBIS; 50-51, Henri Cartier-Bresson/Magnum Photos; 52, © Estate of Jacques Lowe/Woodfin Camp; 54, Bettmann/CORBIS; 55, Royal Canadian Mounted Police © The Crown/JFKL; 56, Courtesy Le Figaro; 57, John Dominis/TLP/Getty Images; 58, Abbie Rowe, White House/JFKL; 59, AP/Wide World Photos; 60-61, Joseph Scherschel/TLP/Getty Images; 62, © Estate of Jacques Lowe/Woodfin Camp; 63, Paul Schutzer/TLP/Getty Images; 64, Hank Walker/TLP/Getty Images; 65, Cornell Capa C/Magnum Photos; 66 & 67, Abbie Rowe, White House/JFKL; 68, Donald Uhrbrock/TLP/Getty Images; 69, Abbie Rowe, White House/JFKL; 70 & 71, Cecil Stoughton, White House/JFKL; 72, Robert Knudsen, White House/JFKL; 74 & 75, © Estate of Jacques Lowe/Woodfin Camp; 76-77 & 78, Cornell Capa

C/Magnum Photos; 79, © Estate of Jacques Lowe/Woodfin Camp; 80 & 81, Cecil Stoughton, White House/JFKL; 82-83, Art Rickerby/TLP/Getty Images; 84 & 85, Cecil Stoughton, White House/JFKL; 86, AP/Wide World Photos; 88-89, Ed Clark/TLP/Getty Images; 90, Robert Knudsen, White House/JFKL; 92, JFKL; 93, Bettmann/CORBIS; 94, Nina Leen/TLP/Getty Images; 95, Stanley Tretick, LOOK Magazine Collection, Library of Congress, Prints & Photographs Division (#LC-USZC4-3272); 96, Hank Walker/TLP/Getty Images; 97, Paul Schutzer/TLP/Getty Images; 98, Hy Peskin/TLP/Getty Images; 99, JFKL; 100, MPI/Getty Images; 101, © 2000 Mark Shaw/MPTV.net; 102, © Estate of Jacques Lowe/Woodfin Camp; 103 & 104, © 2000 Mark Shaw/MPTV.net; 105, © Estate of Jacques Lowe/Woodfin Camp; 106-107, © 2000 Mark Shaw/MPTV.net; 108, Cecil Stoughton, White House/JFKL; 109, © 2000 Mark Shaw/MPTV.net; 110, Cecil Stoughton, White House/JFKL; 111 & 112, Robert Knudsen, White House/JFKL; 113, Cecil Stoughton, White House/JFKL; 114, JFKL; 116-117, Stanley Tretick, LOOK Magazine/JFKL; 118 & 119, Cecil Stoughton, White House/JFKL; 121, Robert Knudsen, White House/JFKL; 122-123, Abbie Rowe, White House/JFKL; 124, Bettmann/CORBIS; 126, JFKL; 127, Cecil Stoughton, White House/JFKL; 128, Alfred Eisenstaedt/Time Magazine, © Time, Inc./TLP/Getty Images; 129, © 2000 Mark Shaw/MPTV.net; 130, Bettmann/CORBIS; 131, Leonard McCombe/TLP/Getty Images; 132-133, © Estate of Jacques Lowe/Woodfin Camp; 134, Ed Clark/TLP/Getty Images; 135, CBS Photo Archive/Getty Images; 136, George Mobley, courtesy WHHA (#2865); 137, George Mobley, courtesy WHHA (#2855); 138, Bettmann/CORBIS; 139, George Mobley, courtesy WHHA (#2857); 140 & 141, Robert Knudsen, White House/JFKL; 142, Cecil Stoughton, White House/JFKL; 143, Abbie Rowe, White House/JFKL; 144-145, Art Rickerby/TLP/Getty Images; 146, JFKL; 147, Cecil Stoughton, White House/JFKL; 148, Abbie Rowe, White House/JFKL; 149, Yale Joel/TLP/Getty Images; 150, Courtesy Princess Irena Galitzine/JFKL; 151, Robert Knudsen, White House/JFKL; 152, Cecil Stoughton, White House/JFKL; 153, CORBIS; 154-155, Bettmann/CORBIS; 156, © 2000 Mark Shaw/MPTV.net; 158-159, Abbie Rowe, White House/JFKL; 160, © Estate of Jacques Lowe/Woodfin Camp; 162, Paul Schutzer/TLP/Getty Images; 163, Charles Moore/BLACK

STAR; 164, Carl Mydans & J.R. Eyerman/Time Magazine, © Time, Inc./TLP/Getty Images; 165, © 1962 The New York Times Company. Reprinted by Permission; 166, Flip Schulke/BLACK STAR; 167, Ed Clark/TLP/Getty Images; 168, Larry Burrows/TLP/Getty Images; 169, Abbie Rowe, White House/JFKL; 170, Keystone/Getty Images; 171, Ralph Crane/TLP/Getty Images; 172-173 & 174, Cecil Stoughton, White House/JFKL; 175, Bettmann/CORBIS; 176, © Estate of Jacques Lowe/Woodfin Camp; 177, Art Rickerby/TLP/Getty Images; 178, Abbie Rowe, White House/JFKL; 179, Bob Adelman/Magnum Photos; 180, Martine Franck/Magnum Photos; 182 & 183, Cecil Stoughton, White House/JFKL; 184, Paul Schutzer/TLP/Getty Images; 185, Ed Clark/TLP/Getty Images; 186-187 & 188, © Estate of Jacques Lowe/Woodfin Camp; 190-191, Cecil Stoughton, White House/JFKL; 192, Art Rickerby/TLP/Getty Images; 194, CBS Photo Archive/Getty Images; 195, Cecil Stoughton, White House/JFKL; 196, © 1963 The New York Times Company. Reprinted by Permission; 197, © 2000 Mark Shaw/MPTV.net; 198, Courtesy Squire Haskins Photograph Collection, The University of Texas at Arlington Libraries, Arlington, Texas; 199, Bettmann/CORBIS; 200-201, Zapruder Film © 1967 (Renewed 1995) The Sixth Floor Museum at Dealey Plaza. All Rights Reserved; 203, Art Rickerby/TLP/Getty Images; 204-205, Carl Mydans/TLP/Getty Images; 206, Abbie Rowe, White House/JFKL; 207, Bettmann/CORBIS; 208, Fred Ward/BLACK STAR; 209, © Estate of Jacques Lowe/Woodfin Camp; 211, Bettmann/CORBIS; 212-213, Elliott Erwitt/Magnum Photos; 214, Loomis Dean/TLP/Getty Images; 215, Robert Lackenbach/TLP/Getty Images; 217, Cecil Stoughton, White House/JFKL; 218, Todd Gipstein/NGS Image Collection.

Photo captions for frontmatter images: Page 2-3, May 11, 1963. President Kennedy during a series of meetings with Canadian Prime Minister Lester B. Pearson. Page 4: The Kennedys pause for a family photo at Hyannis Port, Massachusetts during the summer of 1963. Page 6: March 11, 1963: President Kennedy leaves the State Department auditorium after speaking at a press conference. Page 8: Senator John F. Kennedy speaks in the auditorium of an elementary school during his presidential campaign.

THE KENNEDY MYSTIQUE

Published by the National Geographic Society
John M. Fahey, Jr., President and Chief Executive Officer
Gilbert M. Grosvenor, Chairman of the Board
Nina D. Hoffman, Executive Vice President

Prepared by the Book Division
Kevin Mulroy, Senior Vice President and Publisher
Kristin Hanneman, Illustrations Director
Marianne R. Koszorus, Design Director
Rebecca E. Hinds, Managing Editor
Gary Colbert, Production Director
Carl Mehler, Director of Maps

Staff for this Book
Lisa Thomas, Editor
Judith Klein, Text Editor
Jane Menyawi, Illustrations Editor
Peggy Archambault, Art Director
Jon Goodman, Writer
Lewis Bassford, Production Project Manager
Meredith Wilcox, Illustrations Specialist
Cameron Zotter, Production and Design Assistant

Manufacturing and Quality Control
Christopher A. Liedel, Chief Financial Officer
Phillip L. Schlosser, Managing Director
John T. Dunn, Technical Director
Chris Brown, Manager
Maryclare Tracy, Manager

The Kennedy Mystique: Creating Camelot *is a Partisan Pictures/Blackstrap Productions film. It is available wherever DVDs are sold.*

For information about special discounts for bulk purchases, please contact National Geographic Books Special Sales: ngspecsales@ngs.org

Printed in the U.S.A.

Founded in 1888, the National Geographic Society is one of the world's largest nonprofit scientific and educational organizations. Its mission is to increase and diffuse geographic knowledge while promoting conservation of the world's cultural and natural resources. National Geographic reflects the world through its five magazines, television programs, films, radio, books, videos, maps, interactive media and merchandise. National Geographic magazine, the Society's official journal, published in English and 27 local-language editions, is read by 40 million people each month in every country in the world. The National Geographic Channel reaches more than 260 million households in 27 languages in 160 countries. Nationalgeographic.com averages around 60 million page views per month. National Geographic has funded more than 8,000 scientific research projects and supports an education program combating geography illiteracy.

For more information,
log on to nationalgeographic.com;
AOL Keyword: NatGeo.

NATIONAL GEOGRAPHIC SOCIETY
1145 17th Street N.W.
Washington, D.C. 20036-4688 U.S.A.
Visit the Society's Web site at
www.nationalgeographic.com.

Library of Congress Cataloging-in-Publication Information:

Goodman, Jon, 1952 Aug 20
    The Kennedy Mystique: Creating Camelot: essays/ by Jon Goodman
    p.cm.
    Includes Index
    ISBN 0-7922-5308-6
    1. Kennedy, John F. (John Fitzgerald), 1917-1963—Public opinion. 2. Onassis, Jacqueline Kennedy, 1929-1994—Public opinion. 3. Kennedy, John F. (John Fitzgerald) 1917-1963—Pictorial works. 4. Onassis, Jacqueline Kennedy, 1929-1994—Pictorial works. 5. Presidents—United States—Pictorial works. 6. Presidents' spouses—United States—pictorial works. 7. Public relations and politics—United States—History—20th century. 8. Public opinion—United States—History—20th century. 9. United States—Politics and government—1961-1963. I. Title.

E842.1.G66 2006
973.922092—dc22

                    2005056181

ISBN-10: 0-7922-5308-6
ISBN-13: 978-0-7922-5308-2